Testing and Reclaiming Your Call to Ministry

Testing and Reclaiming Your Call to Ministry

Robert C. Schnase

Abingdon Press
Nashville

TESTING AND RECLAIMING YOUR CALL TO MINISTRY

Copyright © 1991 by Abingdon Press

This book is printed on acid-free paper.

Library of Congress Cataloging-in-Publication Data

Schnase, Robert C., 1957–
 Testing and reclaiming your call to ministry: a practical guide for pastors and full-time Christian workers / Robert C. Schnase.
  p. cm.
 ISBN 0-687-41274-9 (alk. paper)
 1. Clergy—Appointment, call, and election. 2. Church work. 3. Vocation, Ecclesiastical. I. Title.
BV4012.S265 1991
253'.2—dc20   90-48632

MANUFACTURED IN THE UNITED STATES OF AMERICA

To the members and friends of

Wesley United Methodist Church
Harlingen, Texas

First United Methodist Church
McAllen, Texas

Alton Methodist Church
Hampshire, England

First United Methodist Church
Del Rio, Texas

*You taught me what it means
to be a pastor.*

Contents

Acknowledgments

This book is about one of the most noble human aspirations, the desire to serve God in ministry. I am grateful to so many people who have told me their experiences and helped me interpret mine. I am especially indebted to John Platt, Jordan Mann, Bill Hathaway, the late Harold Goodenough, and to my parents, Ronald and Lyla Schnase, for their support and guidance during my formative years. This work never would have gotten off the ground without the compelling encouragement of David Lowes Watson and the insight and honesty of Stanley Menking. I have appreciated my editors, Paul Franklyn and Greg Michael, for their steady guidance. Personal thanks go to Jack and Cathy Radde for providing the perfect place to write, and to Marsha Youker for not allowing me to give up. All these contributed to my enthusiasm; hold none of them responsible for my conclusions.

The most important person in the entire project has been my wife, Esther. She has inspired and challenged, comforted and corrected, and supported me in endless ways. She and Karl allowed me to fulfill this task at the expense of time we might have spent together.

Robert Schnase
McAllen, Texas

A Time of Testing

One Wednesday afternoon when, according to my routine, I went to the hospital to visit parishioners, I ran into Sarah in the hallway. I had seen her before, wearing a pastoral-staff name tag, but this was our first conversation. Happy for the respite between calls, I joined her in her office for further discussion.

Sarah was coming to the end of her ten-week Clinical Pastoral Education program. She was about my age, but her journey in ministry was just beginning, while mine already had rounded the first corner. She told me about the unlikely events that had brought her to the chaplaincy training program.

Sarah, a mother of young children, had felt frustrated with her teaching job and unfulfilled in her limited church involvements. Then she made some hospital calls to fellow church members and had found the experience enriching and powerfully compelling. When she talked with her minister and with a hospital chaplain, they encouraged her to enter the summer program. So, with a mixture of blessing and resistance from her husband, she had courageously signed up for a basic unit of Clinical Pastoral Education at the hospital.

Sarah's Call

During the ten weeks of full-time work and training at the hospital, she visited room to room, comforting families and leading prayers. The experience was entirely new to her. She listened, she cried, she studied. I remember the excitement in her voice as she described the way the experience transformed her: "Now I know that God is calling me; now I feel that I have work to do and am confident about the direction I am going!"

Never had her life undergone such positive change, and never had she felt so richly blessed. She delighted in helping families through crises and found new sources of strength within herself, uncovering talents she never knew she had. Those summer months were the happiest she could remember. She had that glow to her life and bounce to her step of someone who has found joy. The experience of helping, of using her God-given gifts to make a difference in the lives of people—these things affirmed her.

That summer, Sarah became electrified with a call to ordained ministry and soon arranged her life to make that possible. Having set her sights on ways to go to seminary, she asked for her home church's prayers and support, which they generously offered.

Spiritual Depletion

What struck me most deeply about our conversation that day we first met was the contrast between Sarah's spirit and mine. I was at the hospital because it was Wednesday afternoon, and that is one of my scheduled times to visit. She was at the hospital because she found life, vitality, empowerment in those visits. I was there to make calls; she was there because she felt deeply called.

My visits had become routine, but hers were Spirit-led. The work that I described with a deep sigh, she proclaimed with a contagious excitement. Sarah was riding a spiritual high, and the contrast made me painfully aware of my own spiritual depletion. I longed to experience again the freshness and vitality I once had, but which now seemed a fading memory, a flame flickering low. Somewhere down the line, my passion had settled into duty.

Why the contrast? Why did Sarah feel so alive while I felt so dead? Perhaps it was because I was ten years further along than she. I had begun seminary with enthusiasm, my first pastorate with excitement. The natural maturing in ministry may have brought with it a diminishing passion.

But the passage of time alone could not account for all the differences between us. Somehow I had lost touch with my call, and I don't think I fully realized the vital importance of that until my visit with Sarah. My ministry lacked the focus, the intensity, the high commitment and deep confirmation it once had, and all of which I could feel in Sarah's presence. The exhilarating spiritual energy and powerful sense of purpose were missing, had slipped away without my realizing it.

Now in my sixth year out of seminary, I must confess that many times when I visit hospital patients, the fire is not in me. I do not become excited about many things in the usual workday of the pastor of a church. The dreary meetings, the fussy parishioners, the paper-shuffling—I easily lose touch with those flames that flickered in my soul when I first experienced the call to ministry.

What had become of my sense of call? Was it all adolescent illusion and youthful optimism? What became of the flame, the fire, the dynamic spiritual experiences that led me to say I was called to ministry?

Could the call be recaptured and the spirit reidentified through the daily grind of pastoral ministry?

I wonder where that road upon which Sarah entered will one day lead. Through the years of seminary study and learning, what will become of her enthusiasm? Will it continue to be confirmed and strengthened, or will it weaken and wane? Her vision of ministry, as yet untested—will it grow and mature through the complicating factors of salaries and itineracy? The high commitment to God's service—will it withstand the resistance that may come from loved ones? Will the driving love for people be as keen and all-embracing after several years of intensive clinical training? Will her high vision of serving others be strengthened by the spirit-quenching criticisms—and mundane daily tasks—or will it be depleted?

The day Sarah begins to serve as pastor or begins her hospital chaplaincy, will the sense of fulfillment, the certainty about direction, the soundness of the call still be with her? Will the openness to grow, to be led, to struggle still be there? How will she feel about her call ten years from now? Where will she find the strength to endure?

Sarah felt called to the ministry, and most people who enter seminary could relate at least in part to her experience. They had been excited about the possibilities of ministry in one form or another.

Have We Betrayed Our Call?

During the years of parish ministry, what causes dedicated men and women to feel they have lost the spirit that once enlivened them? What causes pastors to wonder if they have betrayed their call?

The period from our initial experiences of feeling called, until we complete the early years in parish ministry is a unique time of testing. The transition from seminary to parish tests our capacity to grow through change. Responsibilities in the church test our skill. Setbacks, criticism, and despair test our spirits. And all these test our sense of vocation, our understanding and perception of God calling us. Through that time of testing, either we develop the spiritual resources that will continue to sustain us as we mature, or we lose touch with our call, and our diminishing sense of purpose fails to sustain us adequately through the trials of ministry.

For the effective and conscientious pastor, the time of testing never ends. Reexamining the call brings rich opportunities for growth, since the original impulses that formed our call at the outset of our journey may no longer be adequate. Testing the call to ministry—a continuing renewal of our sense of call—is our opportunity to mature to a new and more sustaining understanding. Just as the marriage covenant requires continued renewal as the marriage later enters uncharted territory, so our sense of call needs continual reflection and recommitment as we mature in ministry.

By taking a fresh look at your call, I hope you will come to see it as your most important resource for strength in ministry. Part One of this book invites you to recount your original experience of being called and encourages you to consider how you sense the call in your present work. It explores the undercurrents of doubt that threaten every experience of being called and examines the painful transitions in ministry that affect our sense of call. Part Two offers practical disciplines for renewing our sense of call and keeping in touch with the deepest motivations and highest aspirations of our service.

Use the Questions for Reflection at the end of each chapter to guide your personal consideration of the call. You may wish to write out your answers to focus your own thoughts. Or use the questions to guide a discussion group or a retreat on the call to ministry. Encourage other pastors to tell you about their call. The mutual sharing of these questions may serve as one of your best resources for staying in touch with your own call.

If ever we feel we have lost our call, our spiritual vitality, our sense of purpose, even this can be a new beginning toward a more mature experience of God calling us to service. It is vitally important that we examine for ourselves the ways to faithfully follow God, that continuing evocative power in our lives which leads and sustains.

Part One

Testing Your Call

1

Somebody's Calling My Name

The Formative Experiences

The British Methodist Conference, from Wesley's time to today, requires that each new candidate for the ordained ministry stand before pastors and laity to describe his or her call. Without notes and speaking from the heart, candidates tell about the experiences that convinced them that God is calling them. Following the testimony, those listening then ask theological and personal questions about what they have heard.

When I first saw this annual occurrence while serving as a visiting probationary minister, I was terrified! How would I describe my call to the ministry? What would I say? Apart from writing a few brief responses for interview committees, I had never been asked to describe in detail my experience of being called.

The process of asking ministerial candidates to describe their call is repeated, with slight variations, before conferences, synods, presbyteries, dioceses, and congregations throughout the Christian world. By pressing candidates about their theological understanding and personal experience of the call, churches equip their prospective pastors with an invaluable resource for the time of testing ahead.

By the time I began my first pastorate, several years had passed since the original experiences that formed my call to ministry. Through seminary and internship, I had learned many new skills for ministry, and my first pastorate helped me develop those skills to greater effectiveness.

But during many of the most difficult times in the early years, I often found myself asking, "What in the world am I doing here? Why am I putting up with all this? What am I trying to accomplish?"

I discovered that as I develop new skills to answer the how-tos of ministry, I also need a more mature understanding of the purpose of Christian ministry. A timely reexamination of my call, using these questions, keeps my purpose clearly in focus:

- What were the experiences through which God first spoke to me?
- Were the original impulses that caused me to enter the ministry realistic?
- Are those same impulses still active in me today?
- Have I matured to a new awareness of the way God calls?
- Am I still genuinely responding to God's call in my current work?
- How can I keep a vision of the higher purpose through all the mundane tasks and tangles of parish life?

The call, one of our richest spiritual resources, is our way of considering carefully whom we serve, and why. If we lose touch with that call, we lose the higher vision, the treasure at the heart of our faith that makes sacrifice worthwhile and ministry meaningful.

All of you reading this book are capable of recounting

the key experiences in your call to the ministry. I hope my example will cause you to reflect upon some of the events, which, knitted together, formed your own call.

I cannot speak of a single event that marks my call; instead, I can recount many experiences that form the pattern that led me into ministry. No single experience, but a constellation of experiences defines my journey.

A Desire to Help

When I was about sixteen, I joined some other teenagers to chop mesquite to give to poor families for their wood-burning stoves. The welfare office had pinpointed this unusual need and given us names and addresses, and a few of us from the church gave up a December weekend for the task. We drove out to ranchlands owned by a church member and joked and talked as we chopped, our breath smoking in the raw cold.

Then we delivered the wood. The first shack, on the outskirts of town, was set upon a small depression of land that swept down from the railway. We carried the firewood down the ravine through the crisp winter-dried grass and entered the house.

We stood speechless. An overpowering stench stifled our breathing, and the sight, sickening and desperate, stunned us. The north wall was a worn blanket nailed between rotting wooden posts. The east wall was a succession of corrugated tin sheets, wired together like some oversized metal quilt, rigid enough to stand, but loose enough to groan miserably with each howl of the winter wind. The remaining walls were patchwork plywood.

The mother was bedfast with an unnamed illness, and the father, reeking of alcohol, teetered and lurched under its effect. The children—there were several—showed signs of malnutrition. With dulled eyes and emotionless movements, unresponsive to our presence, the youngest sat on the dirt floor, tumbling around with a litter of flea-infested puppies. To one side, dirty dishes balanced precariously.

In the middle of the room stood the wood-burning stove the welfare office had sent us to feed. Our gift of mesquite added to the mixed smells of human excrement, whiskey, and dog food.

None of us knew what to say or how to act. I felt totally helpless. I had never encountered such complete human desperation. At that first home, all I could feel was shock, disgust, revulsion. But then we drove to the second house, and the third and the fourth and the fifth. And when our afternoon ended, my mood had changed. Disgust gave way to pity, pity to compassion. I finished the day deeply troubled, unsettled, angry.

I heard Christmas carols that year in a different key and with a more somber rhythm, sobered by the thought of the way those children experienced the holiday. But mixed with my sadness was a sense of having been addressed, questioned, challenged. The visits to those people evoked from me an unfocused restlessness, coupled with a deep desire for further involvement.

That experience was a spiritual awakening of sorts—not the greatest or the most influential in my life, but one in a long line. I sensed a relationship with people vastly different from myself—a relationship ever so tenuous and slight that had not been there before, but one truer and more real than the separateness that so obviously divided us. I felt I needed to know more, listen more, do more, because of the people I had met and the desperation I had seen.

The only comforting emotion I felt that Christmas was

a mysteriously profound gratitude. I wanted to say to someone somewhere, "Thank you for calling."

I rather doubt that our chopped mesquite brought much warmth to those disheartened homes, but I can bear witness to the small flicker of flame that took light in my heart as I felt a part of something so much greater than myself. At the time, I would not have said that I felt "called to ministry," but the event did help to shape the contours of my faith. Looking back, I can see it as one of the many experiences that molded and formed me, furthered my understanding about myself, and deepened my commitment to God.

Inner Confirmation

When I was a senior in high school, I helped lead a retreat for youth from several churches. I printed the brochure that invited people, arranged for speakers, and worked out the agenda. As part of the retreat, we planned an all-day visit to a center for adults with mental retardation.

I can picture that day as if it were a few weeks ago. We all began the tour feeling uneasy and fearful. The medicinal smells and the eery sound of steel doors locking disquieted our spirits, and the unpredictable responses of the patients flustered what little self-confidence we had brought with us.

But our uneasiness and hesitation melted away within an hour, replaced by a growing compassion for and friendship with the patients. We told stories and listened to sorrows. We played ping-pong and helped with the knitting. We talked about TV programs with people who were desperate for human contact. The residents were as sad as we were to see the afternoon end when finally, through teary eyes, we said good-bye. Several of us

23

signed up to help at the center on weekends, and all of us learned something that day.

When we returned to our church, evening vespers were never so alive and testimony never more sincere as we discussed our experience of serving and helping others in the name of Christ. Many youths discovered that although they went to the center to minister, they returned feeling ministered to.

Personally, I felt a great joy and happiness, born not only of the service we offered the patients, but because I knew that *I* had helped make that possible. I felt deeply that *my* planning skills and know-how had accomplished something important, that God had worked through *me* to make this learning and growing experience possible. The inner joy was profound, the inner confirmation exhilarating.

Mutual Encouragement

After the campfire and singing at another church-youth retreat, a few of us started to talk about God, discussing a Scripture lesson that had been read in the evening devotional. We could not let the idea go; we kept questioning, debating, testing our faith, and as our discussion deepened to new insights, we grew more energetic. We felt like explorers, adventurers in the realm of ideas, voyagers on the sea of faith. Awakened and enlivened by the rich fellowship we shared, we stayed up all night, a night that was cathartic, therapeutic, deeply satisfying.

That was the night I discovered the sustaining strength of community as a dimension of the call, and such experiences have been repeated many times—at other retreats, with other friends, on youth trips, in college cafeterias, and in seminary dormitories.

I have often felt that I am at my best in the world of ideas; that when I share at my deepest, I am giving my most precious gift to others; that when I listen to others, I discern from them some of the most important treasures I will uncover. There is a perception of aliveness, a sense of profound gratitude about meeting together to stir up one another to love and to encourage one another in faith.

Theological Searching

Not all the experiences that formed my call were satisfying. Some were wrought with conflict. I recall a Sunday school teacher who was going through a tangle of personal and emotional troubles. Our high school class was small, with only a few of us present each week. In her search for companionship and stability, the teacher had become part of an extremely fundamentalist group in the community.

One Sunday morning, full of enthusiasm, she announced with a perverse sense of glee that a major earthquake had shaken Central America; this meant that we should rejoice, because all of us were one step closer to the second coming of Christ! The lesson that day covered biblical prophecy about earthquakes and the End Time. I simply could not believe my ears. How could Christians possibly celebrate the death of hundreds of people?

The next morning when I met with the minister, he assured me that the teacher's understanding of Christ's second coming was not the only interpretation of the End Time offered by the Christian faith, and he gave me a book that presented another perspective. For years, I was more clear about what I did *not* believe than what I *did* believe. I clearly did *not* believe that Christ's coming would happen in the manner my Sunday school teacher had described. But it was years before I came to peace with my own interpretation of these matters.

That experience marked the beginning of the search for truth as a dimension of my call, in addition to service and community. All through college, I rejected simplistic understandings of the Christian faith, but I held on to a fundamental belief in the meaningfulness of theology. My task during those years was not to bear some suspicion that theology is meaningless, invalid, insignificant, but that I cannot always understand and see clearly its meaning, validity, and truthfulness.

There must be something to all this theology in general, and to a specific belief in particular, in order to have survived as a sustaining force through all these centuries. With that as a basis for belief, I set out to understand better the Christian faith and my own beliefs concerning it. Thus the evocative power of truth in our search for it became a component of my call to ministry.

Part of Something Bigger

While in college I volunteered to help as a counselor at a suicide prevention center. Each Saturday night for eighteen months, I worked from midnight until eight A.M., listening, comforting, encouraging, and some of those nights were the most frightening I've ever experienced.

I especially recall one night when I talked for five hours with a woman who was closer to killing herself than anyone else I had helped. There was an unspeakable intensity to those hours, riding with her the whole roller coaster of emotions. The fast turns and sudden reverses emotionally and physically exhausted me; few encounters before or since have so pressed my limits of endurance. It took every ounce of energy, every talent for listening I could offer, and every insight into psychology I could recall.

My goal was to see her through the night and get her to professional help in the morning, and only late in the conversation did any light begin to shine in her darkness, or any glimmer come to me that our conversation might help. The story had a happy ending, but it was by no means predictable or assured until the final half hour.

I walked home just after nine in the morning, every muscle aching, my mind feeling as if I had just completed the most demanding final examination of my life.

But when I returned to the dorm, I could not rest. My mind was racing, my spirit was alive. I put on shorts and running shoes, went to the football stadium, and ran around and around the track. It was exhilarating. I was crying, then laughing, then crying again. A deep joy filled my heart. Far from exhausted, I was filled with energy. My feet jogged along with a regular beat, but my soul was dancing, leaping, prancing. My heart pounded with a love for life, love for an anonymous woman whose desperate need helped save my spirit by pulling something out of me I never knew I had.

I sensed that I really matter, that what I do has significance, that God can use me. I felt part of something so much bigger than myself, a small trickle pouring into a running river whose currents are eternal.

I felt addressed, spoken to, commanded. The voice came quietly from deep within, but it was as full and powerful as if the whole universe had spoken to me. I felt as if I were at one with something—perhaps with everything—with myself, with God. I had a mind to think, hands to act, a will to decide, and I had important work to do.

And in my soul I felt profound gratitude and satisfaction for having been found. I breathed deeply the meaning of life, I feasted on its purpose, I tasted its joy. I have seldom had such a deep awareness of being loved and of loving.

A Sense of Direction

God speaking to us—no money can buy it, nothing can motivate us into it but the experience itself, but when it happens, it is worth everything, like the pearl of great price and the treasure hidden in the field.

I could recount other experiences that shaped my soul and from which came my own personal knowledge of the saving grace of Jesus Christ. Through just such simple but profound experiences, an empty life was filled, an imprisoned spirit liberated.

Such experiences did not happen every day, and not always with the same intensity. But they did occur with enough frequency to form a pattern; each new experience was like an additional numbered dot on a child's connect-the-dots picture. At some point while connecting the dots, one begins to discern shape and form, even though the picture is not complete.

My knowledge of Scripture was limited, and I had no theology to adequately express what I was experiencing. The construct of religious call and a response to describe the experiences still seemed foreign to me, but I sensed deep within that I had significant work to do and that God could use me to do it, and I wanted that more than anything in the world.

I began to reflect more diligently than ever about where all this was leading me. And because the experiences were so deeply satisfying, I began to reflect on whether they could become the central dynamic of a person's life, instead of always being peripheral to school, job, career. Could service to people and answers to these inner urgings constitute a vocation, rather than merely an avocation? Could serving God become a lifetime task, not just a part-time hobby?

I began to explore the work of ordained ministry through discussions with pastors. I accompanied them in their work and studied their role. I began to read about ministry and contemplate the call. I could have worked well in another profession, but somehow other alternatives were unsettling to me. I began to arrange my college courses and studies to prepare for seminary. I was not entirely sure what form my ministry would eventually take, but I was convinced that the next step involved seminary. With that decision came a peace and courage I had lacked while contemplating other possible directions for my life.

Called to Ministry

I have just described the initial stages of one person's call to the ordained ministry. Anyone looking at these experiences and my responses from outside the Christian context might use other language to describe what had taken place. For instance, a psychologist might use terms such as teenage psychosexual development, adolescent search for identity, or existential need to be needed. A sociologist might speak about the personal confirmation of cultural values, group adherence, rites of passage, and adoption of role. And all those explanations are partially descriptive.

But the context in which the call occurs—that is, the Christian faith—uses another language to describe my experience, and that language is poetic, metaphorical, powerful, resplendent, time-tested, and sustaining. We are *called* to ministry! These words imply that the joy is not simply of our own creation but comes, gift-like, from beyond ourselves; our service is in answer to a request not of our own asking. The difference we seek to make serves a purpose larger than ourselves, understood only in reference to the life and ministry of Jesus Christ.

I have been asked by some who are struggling to understand their own call whether I ever really heard God speak to me. When we say that God calls us, do we really hear a voice? I must answer ambiguously with Yes and No!

Metaphor is language at its most powerful, poignant and poetic, direct and unencumbered. If we know someone whose strength of spirit never seems to fail, we may say, "Her faith is as unshakable as the earth itself." Or we could speak more directly: "She is a rock." If we have a fleet-footed friend, we may be tempted to say, "He runs as fast as the wind blows." But a metaphor gets right to the point: "He is the wind."

Theologians and poets have always preferred such language to describe reality. David could have written, "As I reflect upon the nature of God, I see that many of God's most important attributes are the same as the qualities of a good shepherd—watchfulness, concern, caring. Further, as I reflect on the nature of humanity, I see that we have many of the same qualities of sheep—helplessness, a tendency to wander, stupidity. Therefore the relationship between God and humans is like the relationship between a shepherd and sheep."

Imagine reciting that at every funeral service! Instead, David used metaphor: "The Lord is my shepherd"— clear, direct, powerful.

The metaphor highlights certain facts about the way people consistently experience God's activity in their lives. The call to ministry as initiated by God is a combination of choosing and feeling chosen, and these experiences are organized in the metaphoric description, "God called and I answered." It often points to the reality that God speaks to us through a series of experiences and people.

Did I really hear God's voice calling me? The answer is No, if you mean I heard a deep, booming, Hollywood voice ringing in my ears—one I could have recorded on a cassette. But if you allow me the full use of metaphor, I say, absolutely Yes. Deep within me and over a period of years, I felt personally addressed. God spoke to me through many people and events. God spoke to me through Scripture, through study, through service, through the church, through times of great joy and periods of despair. In a voice crystal clear on some days; on other days, faintly detectable, God addressed my deepest needs and evoked from me a commitment I really believe I never would have had the strength to make on my own.

Every minister experiences God's call differently. Sarah encountered God's call in mid-life, with a family, while pursuing an established career, and in the specialized area of pastoral care. Her experience differs radically from mine. Yet common themes connect her experience to mine and allow us both to speak with confidence about God's call.

Taking a Fresh Look

Use the following questions to guide your reminiscence about your original call. Write out your responses or share them with another pastor, or with your spouse. One of the most valuable tasks of parish ministry is the reexamination of our call. Yours may be significantly different from mine. Perhaps you experienced it more dramatically or would describe it more graphically. Maybe it came to you over a longer period of time, or later in life, or more suddenly. Perhaps you experienced it more individually or in a richer context of community. Nevertheless, you may recognize some common elements that your call shares with mine, and those common themes are the topic of the next chapter.

=====

Questions for Reflection

Describe your original call to ministry. What key experiences formed your sense of call?

How old were you? How did you feel?

Was there a special worship experience, service project, prayer, Scripture lesson, or hymn that was important?

Who affected your call significantly: a pastor, a layperson, a writer, a youth worker?

What place comes to mind as you reminisce?

How did you experience the presence of God during that period? When and how did you first use the word *call* to describe and organize your experiences?

Who did you first tell about your call? What did you say, and how did you feel? How did they/he/she respond?

How did you tell your family members that you felt called by God? How did they react? What negative responses did you experience? What doubts did you have?

What was the greatest early barrier to becoming a pastor or church worker?

During the time of your original call, what vision did you have of your future ministry? What did you believe Christ wanted from you?

How did you move toward fulfillment of your call? What was the most important advice you received?

How does it feel to reflect on the earliest memories of your call?

2

The Call Reconsidered

Testing the Foundations

Over the centuries, many people have attempted to define the call of God. An exact definition seems so elusive that most attempts finally end with a personal description of what the individual experienced.

Some biblical accounts of the call are quite dramatic. The Bible reports Moses' call in dialogue form. Isaiah encounters rapture in the Temple. God visits Samuel in the night, speaking as clearly as if Eli were calling. Amos has a series of visions. The descriptions are short and concise, and we are left to contemplate for ourselves how those people must have appropriated and reflected upon their experiences.

In the New Testament, we see the disciples respond to Jesus' call. First it may appear that the fishermen dropped everything upon their initial encounter with Jesus. But Luke records that Jesus already knew Simon and his partners before they committed themselves to becoming fishers of men.

Paul sees a vision and hears a voice on the road to Damascus. Some years of reflection followed this dramatic turning point before Paul felt confident and comfortable with his new role. Timothy seems to grow in faith and maturity over a long period of time while traveling with Paul. Even with the more dramatic descriptions, a period inevitably follows during which the person called seeks to sort out the experience to make sense of what has happened.

For us also, the early years of ministry serve as a time to test and confirm our call. Seminaries measure our performance in the functions of ministry and our promise as candidates. But the early years are not merely a time to practice our newly acquired skills. They are also a time to reflect more deeply on the meaning of our call, to confirm the choices we have made, and our responses. During those early years, we should begin a lifelong pattern of continually sorting through our motivations for ministry. This process of testing allows us to reconsider the major themes and distill the essential issues that define our call.

With calls so diverse and experiences so different, we cannot define the call of God with any precision. Nevertheless, it is possible to speak about some enduring characteristics that mark the call of God to Christian service. Take time to reflect on each of the following issues. In what ways are these elements present in your sense of call today?

God Acts First

Our concept of the way God summons people into service comes from the Latin *vocare,* which literally means "to call." From that word we derive such English words as *vocation, invoke, provoke,* and *evoke. Call* is an active-voice verb, so when we invoke the image of a "calling" to ministry, we are raising the question, "*Who* calls?" Who is the principal actor? The language implies that we respond to a summons that we do not create or control. *Call* implies the presence of another, contact with and response to something beyond ourselves and deep within ourselves, in whatever way we understand the nature of God.

The call is not our own doing. There is someone to whom we are responding. Therefore the call does not always lead us to work we would choose for ourselves, if left to our own inclinations.

Sometimes the sense of God acting does not come from how we hear ourselves addressed but from the way we sense ourselves being heard. One minister told me that his call began when he was troubled within and pressured from without. He had a deep sense that there was an Other who heard his pleas, who listened to him, and the presence of that Other evoked from him qualities of character and leadership he never knew he had.

The call does not find its focus in the notion that we expect things from God, but in the sense that God expects things from us for God's purposes. As Paul writes, God "destined us in love" (Eph. 1:5).

There are many voices to which we can respond. Our own egos urge us on in mysterious ways to deeds we do not fully comprehend. Our own unresolved troubles from the past elicit behaviors and responses. The voice of society, the call for the common good, the natural search for significance—all these forces can propel our actions.

But the call of God, even though it might come through specific events and particular people, finds its origins in a deeper source. God's evocative presence, whatever and however God may be, elicits a response that pulls us into a different way of being and doing than we would have arrived at on our own.

Genuine Response

Paul punctuates his prose with such phrases as to the glory of God, "rooted and grounded in love" (Eph. 3:17). When he discusses our work, he constantly admonishes us "not to please men, but to please God," and to work not for our interests but for the interests of others (I Thess. 2:4; Phil. 2:4). "Doing the will of God from the heart" is the highest good (Eph. 6:6). He calls us to truthfulness and away from deceit, and warns against pretenders. Paul understood that a wide variety of impulses shape the human soul, including self-gratification, self-righteousness, greed, and he knew that these cannot sustain the work of ministry. The Christian call to ministry rests most securely on genuine love for God and the sincere desire to serve God as the highest good. The experience of the gracious love of God is the central truth of the gospel, to which ministry is the response.

At issue is the validity of our motivation. A genuine compassion for people or a sincere passion for truth underlie the experiences that form a valid call to ministry. The service we render and the testimony we give flow from deep within, even if at first we cannot adequately express ourselves in solid theological language.

Suppose that when I was chopping wood to give to poor families, some buyers had come along and offered payment for the wood for use in their own fireplaces. How that would have changed the experience! That day would have faded in my memory long ago, instead of serving as a turning point in my journey of faith. *Who* is served makes all the difference. We were motivated by something other than money.

Or suppose that someone had come to me during that

painful night at the suicide-prevention center and promised me an "A" if I helped the caller and an "F" if I failed. Would that have increased my desire to help her? God forbid! My motivations for ministry had nothing to do with grades.

No money could buy the constellation of experiences that formed my call to ministry, and no earthly rewards could have made me work harder. The experience of God's gracious love is desired, accepted, and responded to for its own sake, not as a means to other lesser goods such as wealth, prestige, power, or fame. In my early inner yearnings for a sense of ultimate significance, serving God became the pearl of great price, the treasure hidden in the field.

One cannot properly end a sentence that begins, "I serve the Lord in order to . . . ." One does not serve the Lord because of something else. Serving the Lord, like seeking what is good, is its own legitimacy. At our best, we do not serve the Lord because it pays well, or because it brings prestige, or because someone told us to, or because we were coerced into it, or because we wish to escape the stress of a high-paced business career. We do not respond to the call to ministry because it is the easiest thing to do, or because our parents think it might be best.

We serve the Lord because it is the right thing to do with our lives. Beyond the more limited social, cultural, and familial attainments that shape us, we open ourselves to the infinite and ultimate, connecting our innermost self, our most genuine aspirations, our most unique abilities, our deepest search for significance, to the very ground and source of creation. We serve the Lord as the end and all-encompassing purpose of life.

During the earliest stages of my call, I responded because I felt the desire to serve. I cannot deny that many of my actions might have begun with less than purely Christian motives. Sometimes I was motivated to attend church retreats because I hoped for romantic interludes, or because I simply wanted to get away from my parents for a few days. No doubt I sought some positions of leadership because I thrived on recognition. But the most deeply satisfying events eventually were shaped by sincere motives. Perhaps people called to ministry cannot fully comprehend their experiences or cannot express the meaning of those experiences. These things can be overcome. But the experiences cannot be pretense.

Sometimes people who begin with confused motivations grow into a more genuine sense of call. When I asked an older pastor to tell me about his call, he told me that his father deeply respected ministers and spoke with admiration about their dedication. Also, he said that since he felt his father had always loved his brother more, he had entered the ordained ministry to win the love of his father. However, during seminary, as he became involved in serving people and studying Scriptures, he underwent a "baptism of motivation." No longer needing to prove anything to his father, he continued in the ministry with a true desire to serve God. Self-gratifying motivations were replaced by self-giving motivations.

Genuine love for God must be present sooner or later. Imagine ministry without it. If genuine love for God is absent, we are dealing with people who, at best, are driven by passions they do not control or understand. They are led blindly and naively by ego needs, by vanity, by the need for attention, or by the need to manipulate others. At worst, we are dealing with charlatans, people who purposely act out of self-interest in a malevolent manner.

Christ the Center

Not only must the call to Christian ministry be true in the sense of being genuine, it must be truly Christian, finding its source, context, and confirmation in Christ. The vocation stems from the ministry of Jesus Christ; it flows from the desire to discover more about him or from the longing to follow him more closely.

Paul speaks of the call as a direct response to Christ. We work by his mercy, because of his forgiveness, in response to his grace. Paul believed that our purpose derives from the "eternal purpose which he has realized in Christ Jesus" (Eph. 3:11). Jesus Christ is the source and end of our service, and our duty is to "walk in love, as Christ loved us" (Eph. 5:2).

This criterion is essential. Our Christian faith gives us the language for discussing spiritual realities. If we principally use another language (the language of psychology, sociology, philosophy, etc.) to describe those realities and to interpret the context of our service, we do not have a Christian vocation, even though we are moved to serve our fellow humans. The call to Christian ministry has a distinct context and focus. The paradigm we use for interpreting our experience is God's activity in Jesus Christ and is not derived solely from the social sciences or from purely humanistic impulses.

I do not seek to exclude the usefulness of psychology and the truthfulness of the humanities for understanding our work. Nor am I degrading those people who dedicate themselves to serving people and God through their work in the social sciences. I am not saying that ministry can take place only in a church setting.

I am saying that the interpretive context for validating the call is the Christian faith. By definition, Christian ministry has as its center point, its reference, and its source, a theology of Christ. It focuses on Christ and flows from Christ, no matter how we understand the human condition or the nature of God. If we use another paradigm to explain our intent, or if we use language principally from the social sciences to describe the human soul, we might be doing useful and satisfying work, but we are not responding to the vocation of Christian ministry.

I heard of a psychologist who was asked by a chaplain to serve on the board of directors of a counseling agency. The psychologist, an atheist, told the chaplain he could not serve with an agency which constitutionally requires that all board members must be active church members. He would support the agency, but would not serve as a board member.

The chaplain, an ordained minister, answered the psychologist by saying that he also was atheistic, but he served as a chaplain only because he was trained as a counselor and enjoyed the benefits of the institutional context. The chaplain urged the psychologist simply to overlook the question of church affiliation in order to serve on the board.

The chaplain's lack of integrity appalled the psychologist. The chaplain may serve many hundreds of people as a helping professional, but he lives a lie by using the Christian faith as a pretext in his practice or as a cover for his paycheck, if he does not adhere to its central truth. Vocation that is truly Christian centers on Christ and flows from him.

Uncertainty and Unworthiness

When God called, Jeremiah answered, "I'm too young." Sarah said, "I'm too old." Jonah said, "I'm not inclined." Moses said, "I'm no public speaker." Ezekiel said, "I'm overwhelmed." Isaiah said, "I'm unclean." Amos said, "I'm just a shepherd."

Everyone who senses the call of God experiences doubt, uncertainty, unworthiness. We question our ability to make a difference in the lives of others for God. We doubt whether we have anything worthwhile to offer and the means through which to offer it. We question our own sincerity, our motivations, our worthiness for such a high task. We doubt our own relevance to the gospel task, and at times, we even doubt the relevance of the gospel to the world. Questions arise about our physical and material limitations, the cost and sacrifice to us and to our families. We may face opposition from our spouse and children, our parents and friends and professors.

These doubts provide a natural and responsible way to test the foundations of our call. Absolute and unquestioned confidence about our call may indicate a spiritual blindness or self-deception rather than faithfulness and obedience.

The mystery we wrestle with is that God wishes to use any of us at all. Of all the strange ways for God to reveal unlimited love, God uses limited lives. God speaks an eternal message through temporal creatures; heavenly treasures are placed in earthenware pots. God uses our faltering faith, our partial abilities, our limited perspective, to communicate an all-encompassing vision of new life.

A sense of unworthiness and doubt accompany virtually every response to God's call. The problem is too big, the task too large, the work too strenuous for our paltry abilities.

This doubt within our souls finds sympathy from the resistance we encounter from outside ourselves. The next chapter speaks more clearly about the wily ways and fiery darts that attack our spirit and weaken our faith.

Openness to Others' Needs

God's call to ministry opens us to the needs of others and moves us to respond.

We encounter human suffering. A friend tells us his marriage is in trouble. An acquaintance says her diagnosis is cancer; another, that she has lost her job. Quietly weeping, or remaining stoically silent, a stranger struggles with grief in our presence. At a food bank we see hungry people and witness the hopelessness of poverty.

Human suffering—we hear its cry, we see its tears, we feel its anguish, we touch its wounds—sometimes accidentally, sometimes among friends, sometimes among total strangers. Sometimes it is simple and temporary, at other times profound, enduring, inescapable.

At the moment we face human suffering in any of its infinite colors and textures, a choice presents itself. We are not always fully aware of the choice, and it may be answered intuitively, but it is a choice, nonetheless. Suffering sets before us a decision to be made.

At that moment of decision, if we pay careful attention to our natural tendencies, we discover that we desire to move away. Within us there is the propensity to avoid the pain, to deny the problem. We are pulled in ways we do not understand toward safety, away from human need. Our mind reinforces this tendency by reasoning, "They don't need me. There's nothing I can do anyway. What good could I do?"

But also at that moment of decision, if we listen deep within our soul, we discover that something inside us moves us toward the suffering. Every human soul that harbors the tendency to avoid suffering also houses the capacity to respond compassionately. When we confront need, one path compels us away from the pain; the other evokes the desire to help, a vital aspect of God's call. Opening ourselves to others' needs takes us to uncertain ground and comes with no assurance that all things will work out.

If we open ourselves to need, we experience some uncomfortable moments and awkward incidents. We risk feeling helpless; or worse, we risk sharing the pain of the person who suffers. But it leads to significant growth, and the temporary discomfort is inevitably balanced by the conviction that the experience was meaningful, valuable, even joyous.

Opening ourselves to need is listening to someone speak about divorce without changing the subject, but getting closer, paying attention, sympathizing. It is walking into a nursing home full of rancid smells and hanging in there long enough to show the patient that someone still cares. It is listening as hard as we can to people of different races as they tell us we will never be able to understand them.

The genuine call of God opens us to human need. That one common thread ties together all the experiences that significantly shape the call to ministry. This does not mean we must become perfectly self-giving or that we must experience total self-denial before our call is genuine.

This simply means that those high-point experiences which form the pattern that leads to genuine vocation in ministry find their source in an openness toward need. People who claim that they are called to the ministry, but who always have moved toward the easy and the painless, have missed the mark. The formative experiences, the spirit-led experiences, tend toward service and growth, and direct us toward need, not toward comfort.

Moses could have stayed with the sheep and avoided going back to Egypt. Isaiah could have decided not to upset the powerful rulers of the Judean court. Paul could have walked away from the threats and suspicions of the first Christians he encountered after his conversion. Timothy could have stayed away from the churches that faced controversy and strife.

Throughout the teachings of Paul we find evidence that the call moves us toward people in distress. And in the letter of James, we find: "Religion that is pure and undefiled . . . is this: to visit orphans and widows in their affliction" (James 1:27). In the same epistle, we are admonished to visit the sick, the suffering, the sinful, and the lost. These responses are not possible if we follow only our natural inclinations.

At the crucial moment in our encounter with suffering (*crucial moment* literally means "the moment of the cross"), when we must decide whether to move away or toward it, the call to ministry inevitably moves us toward the pain.

The formative experiences of my call—visiting the impoverished, helping at a mental institution, sharing burdens with friends—all these were easily avoidable. But for responding to God's call in my life, they were essential.

Jesus claimed that Pharisees, always dealing with the clean but never encountering the unclean, were like doctors who avoid the sick. What good is the training if the doctor never meets the sick? What good is a Pharisee's religion, if it never encounters human need? Jesus countered this narrow notion by choosing to open himself to human need, bringing himself constantly into contact with lepers, tax collectors, harlots, and the possessed.

Opening ourselves to the needs of others is not natural. It's awkward. It's risky. It makes us want to know more about people and more about how to help. It leads us to want more tools, more insight, more skills for helping. And in the end, moving toward the need brings life's richest reward, a deep and abiding sense of God's grace, the joy of participating in the coming Kingdom.

Profound Joy

When we open ourselves to the needs of others we also open ourselves to joy. This is the profound satisfaction that comes to us, gift-like, through the service we render, the people we meet, or the truth we seek. This in no way implies that our Christian service always means we are "having a good time." Knowing joy does not mean we get what we want. It is more than a temporary state of contentment.

The impoverished homes we visited to deliver our wood did not make us happy. Anguish and pain marked the night of attempted suicide. Only troubled people would say they have fun when they visit people in their suffering. People are not at their happiest with others who are hurting. Tension, anguish, fear, and foreboding distinguish many moments of great service. But underneath the immediate setting, and deep within the soul, a basic satisfaction, fulfillment, and joy sustain the call to service. The pain of shared suffering must eventually blend with a profound joy in the soul of the minister, in order for service in Christ's name to be sustaining and renewing.

In *Wishful Thinking*, Frederick Buechner describes the call as "the place where your deep gladness and the world's deep hunger meet" (p. 95). The genuinely called have many anguished moments and trying times. But they also have moments of exuberance, of enriching satisfaction, when they share the joy of the prodigal's father, the sheer delight of the treasure finder, the deep gratification of the pearl merchant.

In his letter to the Ephesians, Paul speaks with eloquence about the immeasurable riches of grace, God's kindness, his great love for us, that he made us alive. He writes that we are filled with the fullness of God and can know the peace of God. Beyond Paul's sufferings for the gospel is an even truer reality—that in God, one finds fulfillment and joy.

If we lack joy, then we work as slaves. We cannot render service to Christ for long on the basis of obligation without joy. The soul of the minister who never finds deep satisfaction becomes the breeding ground for resentment and hostility. For effectiveness with the gospel, ministers who merely comply with the job requirements can't hold a candle to those who find their deepest joy and most profound bliss in offering themselves as servants.

Personally Addressed

There is a world of difference between a letter that arrives with our name handwritten and one that is computer-addressed to occupant. The genuine call to ministry comes personally addressed.

My vocation calls for my singular gifts, and it requires the combinations of talent and personality that are found only in me. The call uses what I have learned and what I have made of my own experience. It utilizes my unique training, background, or inclinations.

Paul says, "Grace was given to each of us according to the measure of Christ's gift. . . . And his gifts were that some should be apostles, some prophets, some evange-lists, some pastors and teachers" (Eph. 4:7, 11). Paul clearly believes that God has a purpose for each of us, but what God needs from one person differs from what God needs from another.

There are things others can do that I cannot do because I lack the training, the experience, or the inclination. I should not feel useless because I am not like someone else. God's call does not require that we all fit the same mold.

There are things I can do that nearly everybody can do. These things require no special experience or expertise. Sometimes responding to the call involves doing many things that are so mundane and routine, anyone could do them.

But there are things I can do well that few others can do, and I believe the call usually addresses us in this third scope of abilities. God calls on us to use our mixture of gifts to their fullest. That is one reason the call is so personal.

Moses was called to lead his people out of Egypt. He was uniquely qualified for the job because he was both Hebrew and a member of the Pharaoh's court. Paul was a trained rabbi, a Roman citizen, and had unusual dexterity in the world of language and thought. He was uniquely qualified to bring the good news to the Gentiles.

The place where we grew up, the languages we speak, the quality of our education, the experiences we have had, the sufferings we have endured, our unique personalities, the things we do well and the things we do poorly—all these prepare us to fulfill some duties. The call tells me there is work that I can do that needs to be done.

Some people are uniquely gifted for ministry in rural

areas; others, for inner-city work. Some people are uniquely gifted for work with older adults; others, for work with youths. Some are uniquely gifted to serve in working-class communities; others, in university settings. Part of the struggle of ministry is acceptance of the way our gifts can be used. Our practice of ministry tests us, helping us to see more clearly where God would have us use our personal gifts to their fullest.

Outside Confirmation

Other people must validate, according to their experience and insight, our description of our call and our gifts for ministry. Outward confirmation is just as important as the inward spiritual experience. Otherwise, the church opens itself to confusion.

Even Paul, after receiving the call directly in a vision, submitted to baptism and the laying on of hands for outward validation of his ministry. Throughout his letters, he speaks about the presence of witnesses, public laying on of hands, testing those who are called, and looking at the fruit that each ministry bears. A genuine call requires outside confirmation.

This usually occurs informally at first. Others of the community of faith may say, "Job well done; you have a gift for that; what you do really makes a difference." Confirmation from the community of faith begins with simple praise, sincere appreciation, words of encouragement for the service we render, which confirm our own feelings about our experience.

If we perceive that our call is to ordained ministry, processes begin that offer formal confirmation of the call, concerned with evaluation and accountability, through criteria established by the denomination. The steps involve laypeople, ministers, supervisors, and seminary officials.

Our own personal experience of God's call is not enough. All of us have blind spots, truths about ourselves and our abilities that we do not see. The only way we can insure the accuracy of our vision of ourselves is to test our perceptions with other people.

Our peers in ministry provide a reality test. Otherwise, we might live an illusory life, thoroughly convinced that we have relational gifts and spiritual insights we do not really possess. If the ordained ministry is not for us, interviews and evaluations can save much suffering later on by encouraging us to find other ways to respond to our vocation. We build our house on shifting sand if we try to establish a ministry by using gifts that find no validation from others.

The need for outside evaluation continues throughout ministry. We submit ourselves to our congregations, our denominational authorities, and our fellow pastors in mutual and convenantal accountability. No one enjoys being evaluated, and clear and just performance standards for ministers are difficult to establish and maintain. Unclear or inapplicable standards cause unfair pressure and unreal expectations, especially when applied inconsistently.

But we commit ourselves to obedience through ordination, which requires that we must submit to outside confirmation and evaluation, as imperfect as the performance standards might be. God loves and uses all people to serve God's purposes, whatever their competence, but the church opens itself to destruction if it fails to confirm and evaluate the call to ordained ministry. As long as we feel called to God's service, we lay ourselves open to the confirmation of our ministry by others.

Passion

We must have an active and abounding interest in fulfilling the service of Christ, in loving people, or in seeking after truth. There must be some level of passion, the desire to bring to other people the experience of fulfillment that formed our call, to share the good news, or to render our service in better ways to more people. An ordained minister truly called cannot remain impartial and disinterested when suffering can be relieved, souls comforted, truth expressed.

A woman in seminary gave me a criterion for measuring my interests, a tool for discovering what I most enjoyed.

She simply asked, "What do you like doing well enough that you could stay up all night working on it, without feeling the time pass?" And I realized immediately that some subjects in college totally bored me; preparing papers for those classes led to instant tedium, tiredness, exhaustion.

On the other hand, there were some courses and assignments that I could not stop thinking about and hungered for more. I would delve deeper because I just had to find the answers, and my energy increased the more deeply I dug. This is the sort of zeal I mean. The call to ministry must have some passion and fire.

Luther's Protestants, Calvin's Reformers, and Wesley's Methodists—all were criticized for their enthusiasm, but their high interest in the spiritual and temporal welfare of the people marked them as distinct from many other church leaders of their day. They were eager to do more and to do it better.

Paul used words like *eagerness, boldness, striving.* He criticized idleness. "Be urgent," he said: "Do not be weary in well-doing . . . increase and abound in love; to this end, we toil and strive" (II Thess. 3:13; I Thess. 3:12; I Tim. 4:10). From these phrases and many others, he leaves the impression that passion is characteristic of following Christ's call. That call always includes a certain level of energy, a propulsion for serving God, a zeal for fulfilling God's work.

Pattern Over Time

Many ministers can remember a single significant event that marked the dramatic beginning of their entry into God's service. I am grateful that God makes such powerful changes possible, but a single experience alone does not constitute a call. If the experience is real and God is calling, then the call will be confirmed as well in other settings and in different circumstances.

A vocation, even suddenly and dramatically discovered, takes place only in the context of ongoing growth and maturation. The decisive commitment to follow Christ is both preceded and followed by a developing sense of discipleship, a growth in our understanding of the nature of grace. Our response to God's call is not a once and final decision, but one made repeatedly, sometimes with more clarity and commitment, sometimes with less.

Paul writes, "I press on toward the goal for the prize of the upward call of God" (Phil. 3:14). At other places he describes Timothy's "progress." He reminds Timothy to "rekindle" the gift of God that is within him. His use of *pressing on, progress,* and *rekindle* show that for Paul, the call to ministry was not a single experience but a lifetime of experiences, forever calling for renewed response and commitment.

In geometry it takes two points to make a line. One point leads nowhere. With two, you can conjecture, deduce, and anticipate what may lie between or extend beyond the points. For the call to be deep enough and rich enough to sustain us through years of service and commitment, the sense of vocation must recur many times.

Suppose someone's call includes all the marks listed above. Does this mean that the person is definitely called to the ordained ministry? Not necessarily.

God calls all Christians to the general ministry of the church, and many of the listed characteristics apply as truly to ministry of the laity as to the ordained ministry. Lay people are genuinely called in a personal way to specific tasks.

So even when all the ingredients are present, one must attempt to discern whether the call is to lay ministry or ordained ministry. The call to Christ's service needs further refinement and focus, which comes through study and prayer; further experience and reflection; further correlation of one's unique gifts with special needs.

Unreliable Marks

Many people seem to believe that the ability to preach is a reliable mark of a genuine call. But skill in public speaking, even about God, does not itself indicate a call to ordained ministry.

Others believe that knowledge about theology, or sound moral discipline, or ability to work with youth are reliable marks of the Christian call to ordained ministry. All these may be described as "the gifts of ministry," and they are important. However, not everyone who has the ability to perform some of the duties of ordained ministry should be ordained.

Every significant church founder examined both

outward abilities and inward motivations. When John Wesley inquired after those who would be ministers, his first concern was, "Do they know God? Do they desire and seek nothing but God? Have they the love of God abiding in them?" Next he asked, "Have they gifts for the work?" He wanted both a solid experience of being called and useful gifts for ministry.

John Calvin wrote of the external and formal call which relates to public order of the church, evaluating the gifts and attesting to their usefulness for ministry. But he also wrote of the secret call which the church cannot witness, the internal motivations that drive us to serve God. Calvin acknowledged that without a genuine internal call, we can be motivated by ambition, avarice, and selfishness.

The presence of gifts alone does not mean that one is called to ministry, nor is desire a reliable mark of a genuine call. Sometimes what we want to do is not what we need to do.

Some who dream of one day becoming an ordained minister have an idealistic picture that shields them from the painful, anguished moments, and their desire will not adequately sustain them through difficulty. Others desire to enter the ministry for the wrong reasons, unconsciously needing to be the center of attention, starving for appreciation.

If we follow only our desires and search for our own self-gratification, we risk performing a ministry that is irrelevant to the needs of people and unresponsive to the will of God. The call to ordained ministry requires more than our choice and our will. The notion of the call implies that *God* chooses; it is *God's* will to which we respond.

Unfortunately, even ordination does not necessarily indicate that someone is called to the ordained ministry.

Because the church is made up of imperfect humans, some approved for ordination have never experienced or understood the meaning of the call; they may lack love for God or the necessary gifts to be effective.

Ideally, every marriage license should be proof positive of deep and abiding love, marked by fidelity, commitment, and mutual respect. But we know this is not the case. Likewise, if someone is not genuinely called, ordination does not change that fact.

What, then, is the call? It is the central motivation for all our work. It is the way we understand our purpose. And constant diligence to plumb the depths of our call gives us strength for the times of testing. God acts and we respond. God displays an evocative power, eliciting our response and awakening our desire to serve God by serving others. As one minister shared with me, "I'm definitely here by choice, but somehow the choice wasn't entirely my own."

Questions for Reflection

These ten elements were presented in this chapter: God Acts First, Genuine Response, Christ the Center, Uncertainty and Unworthiness, Openness to Others' Needs, Profound Joy, Personally Addressed, Outside Confirmation, Passion, Pattern Over Time.

Which were present in your original call? Which are you most aware of in your current sense of call? Have you outgrown or lost touch with any along the way? How has your understanding of these elements matured over the years?

How has your sense of call changed? How has your experience of God changed? Are your motivations for continuing in ministry different from those you had when you entered ministry?

How do you view the relationship between what you do in your work and what Jesus Christ did during his life? What experiences make you feel you are accomplishing the work of Christ? What important needs do you feel you are addressing?

What do you find most fulfilling about your work? How do you see your future in the ministry? From what is that vision derived? Do you ever sense that your will for your future conflicts with God's will? How do you resolve the conflict?

How does your call find informal confirmation today? What kind of formal confirmation do you receive through evaluation? How do other pastors view your ministry?

Are you doing what you do today in response to God's call?

3

Wily Ways and Fiery Darts

Tests of Spirit

Put on the whole armor of God, that you may be able to stand against the wiles of the devil. For we are not contending against flesh and blood, but against the principalities, against the powers . . . against the spiritual hosts. . . . Stand therefore, having girded your loins with truth, and having put on the breastplate of righteousness, and having shod your feet with the equipment of the gospel of peace; besides all these, taking the shield of faith, with which you can quench all the flaming darts of the evil one. And take the helmet of salvation, and the sword of the Spirit, which is the word of God.   —Ephesians 6:11-17

Target Practice

When I first announced my intention of entering the ministry, my father told me, "You'll never make enough money to support yourself. You make good grades. You could do anything you want. Go into science or medicine."

A friend said, "You? A minister? No way. That's crazy. You can't be serious. Nobody who's sane does that these days."

An English professor who appreciated my work turned against me when he heard the news: "Nobody with a modern mind can believe that stuff. I'm disappointed in you." On one of my next papers, I described something as "peaceful." Written in red was the comment, "Where did you get that from—an old gospel hymn?"

My philosophy professor wasn't worried. She simply said, "One day you'll grow up, and with maturity, you'll put all this nonsense behind you."

My fiancee's mother was overheard lamenting, "What worries me is that neither of them has the personality for the ministry. Neither of them is outgoing enough. They'll spend all their lives moving every couple of years."

While we were unloading the moving van at our first church, a woman from the parsonage committee talked incessantly about the minister who had just moved out: "Now, he was a real gospel preacher! No one will ever fill his shoes. It will never be the same without him."

After one family left the church, my predecessor told me, "It doesn't surprise me that they left. They were always strongly in my camp. I didn't think they'd like you."

To every new idea I considered, the church secretary would respond, "It sounds pretty crazy to me. That will never work. There's just no way. I suppose you could try it, but I can tell you that people will get pretty upset."

One day in the grocery store, I ran into a member whose attendance had fallen off after my arrival: "Oh, don't worry about us. It's just that the previous minister was our friend, not just our pastor. You'll make friends too, sometime."

At a pastors' meeting, another minister took me aside to say angrily, "I'm fifty-five years old, and it makes my stomach churn to see someone in his twenties serving a bigger church than mine. The only reason you got that church is because you're the superintendent's pet."

The next-door neighbor called my wife to ask, "Is there some committee at your church that I could call to complain about how high you let your grass grow in your backyard?"

Feeling left out after a Christmas party that all our friends had been invited to, I later found out why we were not included: "We wanted to invite you, but we didn't know what we would do about serving alcohol. We were afraid to offend you."

When I served as a character witness at a trial, the opposing attorney attacked my testimony: "How can we trust the word of someone in the ministry? He obviously sees only what he wants to see. It's not like he's a psychologist."

A woman who works with refugees came into my office: "I understand your church has no mission." When I outlined several of our outreach projects, she answered, "Those are just garbage. Unless you're on the front line with refugees, you are no pastor at all."

With unendurable frequency, some church member would storm into the office to say something like, "We found drawer number two in the kitchen unlocked, and some of the forks were in the spoon drawer. Who's been in there? Why can't you people keep track of these things? That's your job!"

Church attendance began to increase, but one key church leader commented at the board meeting, "Yes, attendance is up. But you can't count that. They're all visitors."

We set an attendance record one Sunday, and I was walking on air until one member said, "Why doesn't anyone have any joy in this church? Nobody's happy here. I looked at all the faces during Communion, and they're all sad. This church is dying."

When I entered a nursing-home room, a parishioner welcomed me with, "Finally. It's been so long, I'd nearly forgotten what you look like."

One pillar of the church complained, "We don't need sermons about justice. What we need are good sermons against homosexuality and about the Virgin birth. The growing churches stick to the fundamentals of God and country."

After we had slipped up on the newsletter prayer list, the phone rang and I heard an angry voice: "If there was ever a time I needed prayer in my whole life, it is now. I'm sure that's why I'm still sick. Why do you try to hurt me?"

While meeting to plan the details of a funeral, I was instructed by one of the family members, "We don't care what you say. Just get it over with quickly."

During those early years, I also received many words of encouragement that strengthened my spirit. I do not dwell on those because you will have no trouble dealing with them. Receive them when they are offered, and hold them dear for the treasures they are.

Fiery Darts

Part of growing up in West Texas has to do with learning about the different varieties of cactus. Generally, we learn about a new species when we are stuck by one. I spent many painful summer afternoons extracting thorns from my fingers and feet. The most painful kind were those that not only pricked the skin but poisoned the wound. That irritating burning sensation lasted long after extraction of the cactus spine.

I hope the list which began this chapter gives some indication of what I mean by fiery darts. While the list is long, it is only partial. One night when I had trouble sleeping, I wrote out seventy-five of those fiery, flaming little darts in just thirty minutes.

Sometimes the darts come from nowhere, like sniper fire, an unpredictable guerrilla warfare. Other times, I face a battlefield full of dart throwers, taking aim with zeal and obscene pleasure. Sometimes spies infiltrate my own camp and attack me through the people I love and trust, my closest allies and most intimate confidants.

Some of these darts elicit immediate anger. Many leave me floundering and frustrated. They make me want to show people what's what, argue back, fight it out.

I am provoked to shout angrily within my soul, "Why am I fooling with this kind of stuff and these kinds of people? Why should forks in spoon drawers and comments about my predecessor derail my momentum? If only these people and their comments wouldn't encumber me, I could get on with significant ministry."

Paul used the image of flaming darts to describe the attacks that sap our strength and debilitate our spirits. He says these darts originate with the wiles of the devil. His use of the word *wiles* indicates that the spiritual attacks upon our soul feel as though someone somewhere is purposely contriving, strategizing how to wound us in just the right place. He makes it sound as if there is a conspiracy. The attacks are not random, but seem calculated, as though the archer were aware of our most sensitive spots.

Paul says we are not contending against flesh and blood. Our enemy is an interior one, our battle a matter of spirit. In other words, the one from whose lips the flaming darts spring is not the true enemy. The carrier of the biting message is only the vehicle, the temporary transmitter for the wily one. Even if we wrestle the carrier to the ground, we savor no victory, because the real battleground is within ourselves; our troubles are tailored to suit our spiritual vulnerabilities.

At times I have despaired, thinking that if I really were called to ministry, I would not be vulnerable to such attacks. But these are the challenges every pastor faces daily, and an understanding of these spiritual struggles is part of our journey toward maturity in ministry. Such struggles test us and help to form us. Our commitment to Christ is forged through such experiences. They keep the question about whom we serve fresh before us. They can even become openings for growth in understanding ourselves, our motivations, our call.

Penetrating Poison

Here we are exploring the underside of the call to ministry. Every pastor encounters external resistance and internal doubts. Each one faces times of spiritual malaise, bogged down by a sense of inadequacy, unworthiness, frustration. The hurting comments people make and the failures we experience combine with our own doubts about our call, and the combustible combination is soul scorching.

The damage done when these wounds receive no salve is long lasting and cumulative. Without treatment, the poison penetrates to all levels of life. I began my first pastorate enthusiastically, but I soon learned how much more easily I catch congregational despair than the congregation catches my enthusiasm.

To complete the assault, add the guilt every minister begins to feel about falling behind in visiting the elderly. Augment the attack with the discomfort about taking days off when we know there are so many unfinished tasks. Strengthen the siege with the incessant omnipresent pressure of preparing sermons, then add a few anguished Saturday nights mixed with the growing temptation to copy other preachers' sermons. Don't forget the strafing of doubts about whether our gifts are really adequate for our responsibilities and the guilt about not spending enough time with the family. Flaming darts and wily ways. Somebody is conniving to get us.

Like most ministers I've known, I went through a period of depression early in my ministry. I felt emotionally exhausted. My sense of personal accomplishments diminished; the inner flame of compassion flickered low. I began to blame church members for all the problems, feeling hostile about their criticism and critical of their flaws. I fell victim to the "us and them" language when speaking of church staff and church members. For several months I served a fortress ministry, coming to the office each morning with the dread of someone heading for the battle trenches.

And when I didn't blame others, I blamed myself: "They're right. I'm no good at this work. Something is wrong with me. A good pastor doesn't encounter this kind of resistance." I thought I was the only pastor who faced such troubles, that the attacks on me were entirely unique.

I gained twenty pounds and, for the first time in my life, began to show symptoms of high blood pressure. Apparently my perfectionist personality tends to internalize criticism until I become my own worst enemy. Even when things were clearly on an upswing, I could see nothing but negatives. If we set an attendance record Sunday morning, that evening I would wonder why the Jones family hadn't been present. If anything was wrong, everything had to be wrong.

Many people at this point in the downward spiral are vulnerable to alcohol abuse or tranquilizer overuse. Stress to the point of burnout causes chronic tiredness and susceptibility to illness.

Why do these comments debilitate me? Why do the negative comments still sting, long after encouraging comments have ceased to bolster me? What gives the wily one the power to make me question my call to ministry?

During my first few years especially, I viewed the struggle as a battle with an external enemy. When people challenged my decision to enter the ministry or criticized my work, I responded with anger. I heard their comments as an external test of my abilities.

I thought, "If I prove to them how fine a minister I am, then their criticism will stop, and they'll respect and love me as I deserve. If I bring in enough new members, and get the spoons and forks in the right drawers, and edit the newsletter prayer list more carefully, and make more home visits, then criticism will cease."

I nearly ran myself ragged before I realized I was pursuing a receding goal. No minister can do enough to please everyone; no pastor can win everyone's love. No one can control everything that goes on in the church, and the attempt to do so kills the spirit even faster than the flaming darts.

Recurring Themes

After those few exhausting and exasperating years when I tried to outmaneuver the wily one and his barbs by seeking to please everyone, I began to face the real enemy and name the demons. I realized that in my own life, there are certain recurring themes to the devil's wiles.

Need to Achieve

Some of the comments that hurt me most are those that challenge my sense of accomplishment. I really desire to make a difference in this world, to have an impact, to do something worthwhile. And part of that desire is to do something that other people will see and value. I want my parents and in-laws and professors and peers and the lay people to think that I am doing something important. Perhaps that is why some ministers are seduced into leading unnecessary building projects. How wonderful to be able to see concrete evidence of our work, measurable marks of our contribution!

But sadly, most of the work of ministry does not produce results that are widely appreciated and valued.

Many of the fiery darts hit me squarely at that point of vulnerability. They give voice to doubts I harbor within my own soul—terrifying doubts—about the nature and purpose of the work to which I've committed my life. Is the cause really worthwhile? Where are the concrete results? What have I achieved?

Jesus must have had some of these thoughts when he faced the tempter in the wilderness and was offered the chance to change stones into bread. Have you ever considered what you would do if you were offered that opportunity? Sometimes I would give anything to be able to turn stones into bread. I work in one of the poorest counties in the United States, a terrain with an unending supply of stones. To use them as bread would make such a difference! How great it would feel to know how many hungry people I was feeding! If I could find the solution to world hunger, then I'd show all the people who worry about my success, and all the others who think ministry is no longer useful!

Why did Jesus say no?

Need to Be Loved

Other comments that strike me most painfully are those that make me question just how well-liked I am. I need approval from others. I enjoy applause and compliments and awards and other kinds of strokes. I want loved ones to be pleased; I want other ministers to respect me; I want supervisors to appreciate me and parishioners to love me. I thrive on positive response!

When people say they are not impressed, that they are disappointed, the fiery darts strike to the heart. The wily one nails me again!

How dare those church members like my predecessor better than me! This attitude sounds childish, but any honest minister will confess to such feelings. We derive our sense of self-worth from what we do, and when what we do does not impress people, we take it as personal rejection.

The struggle to impress and the need to be liked must have been at the heart of Jesus' temptation to throw himself down from the temple top. How impressive that would have been! Can't you feel the suspense, hear the gasps, see the wide-eyed crowd? Can't you imagine the applause, the publicity? People would have talked about Jesus and his dazzling ability. He'd be liked and popular. He'd be in demand!

Why didn't he do it?

Need to Control

A third theme runs through the list of flaming darts. When the wily one wants to strike me again where I am vulnerable, he attacks my need for control. I want to know what's going on throughout my congregation. I want to be able to influence all outcomes. I tend to feel personally responsible for all that goes on in the church—from attendance patterns to which drawers the spoons are in.

In theory, I preach of a shared ministry. In practice, I want things done well, and the only way I can assure quality is to control things myself.

Comments that challenge my illusion of control remind me that all things are not the way I want them, that some things go on that are contrary to my personal wishes. Some things around the church are not working perfectly according to *my* plan.

Perhaps I struggle in an infinitely smaller way with the same temptation Jesus encountered when he was offered all the kingdoms of the world. Then he could have ruled the world with unquestioned authority. He could have set the kingdoms exactly on the course he wanted them to follow.

Why didn't he accept that offer?

Spiritual Defenses

It is no coincidence that the story of Jesus in the wilderness describes three temptations similar to my struggles with the wily one. The story represents a distilling of the most essential tests to God's call that our faith records.

Our salvation is in that story. As Jesus stands firm against the wiles of the devil, he shows us what is really at stake as we test our call to ministry.

First, we must face the real possibility that pursuing the need to succeed in a worldly way, the need to please others, the need to control everything in the church, may not be following the call of God, but listening to the voice of temptation. Jesus saw through the wily one and was wise enough to discern that turning stones to bread, tumbling from the temple, taking control of all king-doms, ultimately meant that he was serving himself rather than the God who called him to obedience. Our spirits wither and die when we confuse the call of God with the call to achieve in a worldly way, to please others, and to control.

Second, the story reminds us that we need to constantly reconsider which voice we're going to follow. Who are we really going to serve? Ourselves? Our own need to achieve, to be loved, to control? Or do we serve God? The flaming darts give us occasion to consider this question again and again. Answering God's call to ministry is not a once-and-for-all experience. The soil must be constantly retilled. The fiery darts keep us on our toes, perpetually attentive to subtle tendencies to serve other masters.

Third, the story reminds us that the real source of our self-worth is that Christ loves us and redeems us. The grace leading us and working through us is our only hope. We will never be successful enough, or liked enough, or have enough control to bring about the kingdom by our own efforts. In the ministry, we live by grace or we do not live at all.

After Paul objectifies the personal pains by calling them flaming darts, he admonishes us to put on the full armor of Christ as our protection against the wiles of the evil one. Our armaments are truth, righteousness, peace, faith, salvation, and the Word of God. These armaments are the spiritual resources which we perilously neglect; the enemies are spiritual hosts, principalities, and powers. Our only hope is to keep alive the faith with which we first began our journey; to do what is necessary to nurture those relationships and develop those disciplines that help our faith mature so that we can withstand the wily one at every stage of ministry. When we lose touch with the spiritual resources, we are left defenseless.

We are fortunate to live during a time of relative peace and comfort for the Christian church in America. The challenges to our spirit which test our call, and the things that frustrate and anger us in parish life seem so mild and weak when compared to the flaming darts experienced by Paul and his companions. Those fiery darts were arrests, riots, mobs, beatings. They burned out their lives in service to their Lord. We should hope that we have inherited enough of their spiritual strength to withstand attacks about forks in the spoon drawer.

The flaming darts test us from the moment of decision, at the earliest response to God's call, and they continue until breath itself leaves us, until we finish our course in faith and rest from our labors. God's voice may call us in a whisper that only the sensitive spirit can detect. But you can bet that the shout of the wily one hardly requires a well-tuned ear. The wily one's voice is piercing, thunderous, excruciatingly well-orchestrated.

Questions for Reflection

What kinds of experiences may make you reconsider your commitment to the ordained ministry?

What are your greatest doubts about your call and ministry today?

What resistance most acutely challenges your call?

What are the recurring themes in your own spiritual struggles? What depresses you? What kinds of comments hurt most?

How do you distinguish constructive criticism from senseless attacks on the spirit?

In what ways do your needs to achieve, to please others, to control, serve as spiritual hazards?

With whom do you share your painful moments? How do you handle criticism? Evaluation?

What are your sources of self-esteem? What are you most proud of? What are you most defensive about?

What relationship do your spiritual struggles have to Jesus' temptations?

4

Culture Shock

Tests of Transition

My wife and I worked in Great Britain for a year, and we shall never forget those early weeks in a foreign country. The British spoke the same language, yet the accent and word choice confused us. The move shattered our routines, and even the simplest tasks, such as counting money and grocery shopping, took our full concentration. We would return from each little encounter exhausted, often frustrated that we could not make our thoughts clear to others.

Our hosts treated us kindly and sympathetically, but they could not know how difficult some routines were, how different British life seemed to us. At the beginning we often felt quite alone. We missed our closest friends painfully and began to wonder why we had left home at all!

I have just described culture shock—the disorientation, frustration, loneliness, and depression that accompany the abrupt move from one set of relationships, routines, and standards to another. The stress that comes with sudden transitions saps strength and exhausts personal resources. People who move from one culture to another spend so much time adapting to the changes and adopting new habits for survival that they often lose sight of the original purpose of their work in the new land.

Corporations with overseas offices know the hazards, and they develop programs to help their employees through the transitions. The most helpful programs explain some of the differences that workers encounter in the new situation and describe some of the emotional responses they can anticipate. No one can entirely eliminate the feelings of culture shock, but consultants can offer practical suggestions for coping.

For my wife and me, the transition from seminary life to parish ministry was as traumatizing as the move from one country to another. When we arrived in England, we expected major differences and anticipated some of the disorientation. But we did not foresee as clearly the struggles and emotional stress that would accompany the transition from campus to congregation.

Ministerial culture shock takes many forms. The mid-life change of careers, the move from solo pastor to staff member, the change from rural ministry to city parish—all abruptly take us from one distinct way of thinking and relating and functioning to another, and all leave us vulnerable to the effects of culture shock. Even the move from one parish to another, which every minister experiences, can cause this stress. The routine week in one setting contrasts sharply with the work week in another, and the relationships shared with church members in a new congregation can never replace the relationships cultivated in the old.

The move from seminary to parish will illustrate the stress that comes from any major transition in the ministry. The way we cope with this important transition can affect the way we experience transitions throughout our ministry.

Each year thousands of seminarians and spouses move

from seminary life to parish ministry. Some handle the transition more smoothly than others, but all have their spirits tested by the stress and disorientation. Let's begin by considering some of the cultural differences between the seminary environment and the parish community.

Roles

After graduation, I loaded our moving truck as a student; two days later, I unloaded it as The Pastor. I had bundled our boxes while dressed in cut-off jeans and a T-shirt full of holes, surrounded by friends, joking about our haphazard packing and complaining about the heat. I unloaded our truck in the presence of three well-dressed ladies from the Parsonage Committee, come to catch the first glimpse of the person who would perform their daughters' weddings and conduct their friends' funerals. No jokes, no cut-offs, no complaining aloud. Esther and I found the contrast in our behavior and mood striking and disconcerting.

Roles change dramatically when a student becomes The Pastor. In seminary, peers and professors regarded my opinion as just one of many diverse opinions. I enjoyed a certain anonymity. No one paid much attention to my coming and going, and few cared how I dressed or whether I shaved. I could attend any meetings with any group I chose, and no one noticed. Single students could date anyone they wished, and anyone could attend any movie.

My role as The Pastor differed remarkably. Rather than one among many, my viewpoint about a community activity or a theological issue had a special authority. What I said and how I behaved mattered more to other people than it did even to me. My word in the church had more power to influence or to distress than it did in seminary. And since I had learned to follow the directions of professors, I found myself awaiting instructions from the lay leaders, while the laity waited for authoritative approval from the pastor before proceeding with a project. Seminary taught me to follow, but the laity expected me to lead. Seminary taught me to complete assignments on my own, but in the church, I needed to define assignments in cooperation with others.

My primary role in seminary and college was to receive. Courses, guest lecturers, special programs, community activities, and chapel services usually were presented by others to nourish and benefit me. But when I began my work in parish ministry, my primary role was to give. I planned classes, programs, community gatherings, and worship primarily to serve others. I liked that, but with the change in roles I also missed being the recipient.

Whereas I was blessed with anonymity as a student, I was cursed by high visibility as the pastor in a small community. Suddenly people noticed every move I made. In grocery stores, gas stations, cinemas, I encountered people who knew me, and they conveyed their impressions of me to countless others after each conversation. My coming and going became a topic of interest, and the way I dressed or shaved seemed terribly important to a surprising number of people. I moved from the peripheral existence—as one of many—to center stage, the only pastor those church people had. The personal habits of ministers concerning alcohol, tobacco, or dating, which interest few in seminary, in the parish become almost everybody's business.

Ministers who strive only to fulfill other people's expectations eventually feel compromised and angry that they cannot live their own lives. They shop in neighboring towns to conceal some of their personal habits; they drive long distances before letting their hair down and being themselves. Ministers who insist on living just as they please and expressing their opinions as openly as they did in seminary usually end up hurting people they never intended to offend. A pastor's casual criticism of the current presidential administration, which excited no fellow students in seminary, may alienate church members who worked many weeks to get that person elected. Students' adjustment to the difference in roles when they become pastors affects both their own sense of well-being and their relationship to the congregation.

Relationships

Relationships with the laity in the parish differ remarkably from relationships to peers and professors. This adjustment presented us with the most problems.

In seminary, my wife and I felt sustained by close bonds with others. Friends and neighbors with common interests and concerns surrounded us. Our friends were about our own age, shared similar educational backgrounds, and we all lived together in the same student-housing complex. We shared the same flexible hours of study and play, saw each other in class, at supper, in the dorm, in the library, and at the jogging track. And, as if in anticipation of the separation to follow, these relationships tended to grow more intense as graduation approached, sharpening the contrast between seminary and parish life. Many whose love and friendship had sustained us most moved hundreds of miles away upon graduation.

In contrast, we found ourselves, like many first-time pastors, appointed to a church with few people our own age, and even fewer with similar educational backgrounds or interests. No one lived just down the hall anymore, and when we did meet people with like interests, work schedules militated against get-togethers for supper or movies. I had no one around for those stimulating, vituperative late-night theological discussions, and we missed the togetherness of weekly dinners with friends. We often felt as if we initially had to hide part of ourselves in order to make friends, never revealing what we thought theologically, and seldom commenting on books we had recently read. For a time, we grieved with all the attendant emotions that come with losing loved ones.

Pastors who seek relationships in the parish which replicate the friendships they had in seminary may enter dangerous waters. New pastors must show some caution about choosing their confidants. They may be tempted to share vocational discomfort and theological doubts as they once did with a professor, seeking insight and advice. But trusting a particular church leader with that openness may be asking more of that leader than he or she can give. And strong relationships with one group in the church too soon may alienate another group. New pastors must develop sustaining and trusting relationships in the parish or their spirits will wither and die, but they must carefully consider that the parish context differs from that in seminary.

Work Structures

In the transition from seminary to parish, one moves from a highly structured environment to a situation with far less structure. This surprised me. After all, I thought, isn't seminary life rather unstructured, with everyone studying according to his or her own schedule, some late at night and others early in the morning?

Think again. In seminary, professors assigned specific work with clear expectations, a stated deadline, and an agreed method of evaluation. For years I had answered to bells not of my own ringing and accepted tasks not always of my own choosing. Although study time and play time seemed flexible, that flexibility was within limits carefully defined and rigidly structured.

On the other hand, no one assigned tasks or structured my time in the parish. I acted as my own boss and no one else disciplined my schedule. I decided whether to study for my sermon on Tuesday, Thursday, or Saturday. I determined whether to visit three families, or eight, during the week. Except when emergencies arose, I planned whether to fill Friday morning with paperwork, or with program preparation, or with counseling.

This may not seem too difficult an adjustment, but this difference accounts for as much stress as any other transitional factor. Ministers who have difficulty creating structure for themselves soon feel overwhelmed by unfinished tasks, swallowed up by unmet obligations. They will retreat into paperwork in their search for structure, exhaust themselves by late-night sermon writing and early-morning prayer breakfasts, and find themselves spiritually depleted from "lack of time" for prayer and personal reading. It is easier to follow a structure set by outside authorities than to develop the discipline necessary to work effectively as manager of our own time. However, a less structured environment does allow for greater personal creativity, if it is disciplined and managed constructively.

Sources of Self-esteem

I found that in the parish, my own sense of self-worth and self-confidence depended upon different factors

77

than in seminary. This was a difficult but significant idea to comprehend, and I paid the cost in unnecessary depression and a deep sense of failure for overlooking this insight.

Despite the fact that we preach that salvation is by grace, we tend to tie our sense of self-worth to our accomplishments, rather than basing it on the fact that God creates and loves each of us uniquely. We maintain self-worth by a confidence in our abilities, and we therefore assume that our abilities are revealed through our performance or our work. When others criticize our performance or our work is incomplete, we begin to doubt our ability. When we question our ability, our sense of self-worth erodes, and when our sense of self-worth crumbles, the clouds overcome us and the storms beat against our door. The result is depression, a feeling of uselessness, a sense of failure.

What does this have to do with the transition from seminary to parish life? Although not immediately obvious, this has *everything* to do with how we feel about ourselves during the change. Seminary sets before us well-defined expectations in the form of course assignments and tests. We complete the term paper or examination, and receive our evaluation quickly, according to clear criteria. Whether we pass or fail, we know exactly where we stand. The semester ends, we take a break, then begin the process all over again. Through grade school, high school, college, and seminary, this routine of academe runs through our hearts and souls.

But in the parish, I found no clearly defined expectations. No one said how many visits I must make to achieve an A, or how much paperwork or counseling deserved a B. No one evaluated me clearly, directly, or immediately. Evaluation was more subtle and ambiguous, and far less trustworthy. I didn't know whether to believe the woman who told me each week that my sermon surpassed any she had ever heard, or the critic who grumbled about every pastor who had served the church during the past thirty years.

And unlike seminary assignments, most church programs never come to a clear conclusion. Visitation is never finished, and church financial needs continue without end. Unlike my student days, I never knew exactly where I stood. I constantly looked for messages from church members to answer my questions: "Am I doing the job well? What is the job I'm supposed to do?" My performance and ability were never clearly evaluated in ways that fully sustained a sense of self-worth, and this ambiguity caused me to doubt my effectiveness even during successful programs. It compelled me to seek every possible positive stroke or compliment to reassure myself of my own usefulness.

In addition, the skills rewarded by seminary are different from those rewarded by the parish. Seminary rewards functional skills—writing, researching, thinking, planning. But parish people appreciate interpersonal skills—friendliness, leadership, caring.

Pastors who still maintain their self-worth principally through functional skills will engulf themselves in paperwork and program planning and sermon writing, and perhaps do fine work, but they will not feel as rewarded as they think they deserve. Visiting, attending Sunday school parties, and getting along with children may count as favorably in the parish as a well-organized financial report that takes hours to complete.

Furthermore, church members experience a weakness in functional skills as a relational shortcoming. For instance, if the pastor overcrowds the schedule and cannot visit Aunt Martha at that time promised, Aunt

Martha and her relatives will not interpret this as a sign of poor time-management skills. They will experience the pastor as uncaring and inconsiderate.

If we continue to derive our sense of self-worth from the accomplishment of the sorts of tasks we mastered in seminary, we will find ourselves frustrated by the congregation's lack of appreciation for our work. The accomplishments that sustain our sense of usefulness differ dramatically as we move from seminary to parish, and the deeper our understanding of these dynamics, the more we can protect ourselves from unnecessary discouragement.

Faith Perspectives

Seminaries generally encourage an openness to new ideas and reward a searching, growing faith, but local church members often desire certain answers and sure leadership about faith issues; they have more respect for authoritative responses to questions about the Bible. Seminaries frequently encourage interest and activity in social issues for which local congregations share little enthusiasm. Seminarians often belittle the simpler or more fundamental faith of some local church members, while churches in many parts of the country criticize seminaries for their liberal ideas.

I felt caught in a bind during many Bible studies in the local church when people asked what I thought about a passage. On the one hand, I felt it important to explain my understanding of the Scripture, even though it might be quite different from their own. On the other hand, I feared any confrontation that might result among those who had little tolerance for opposing interpretations. Sometimes I felt guilty about hedging on such important issues; at other times I feared I might cause someone else to stumble.

I also felt a tension between my public faith-sharing— in teaching and preaching—and my private faith-sharing with someone who brought up questions that flowed from an inquiring mind and sincere struggle. As I shared privately some of my personal understandings of the Christian faith, including some doubts and unresolved questions, often the person would ask, "Why don't you preach about these things?" And I began to question my theological integrity. Should my public faith-sharing be the same as my private faith-sharing? Or should I continue to preach what I know, saving questions about what I doubt for those who can handle ambiguity?

I also discovered that the biblical and social issues that interested me and sustained my vision of ministry frequently did not match the issues that mattered most to the laity of our church. In a study of the story of Noah during my first months in the pastorate, I researched the place of the story in the Christian tradition, the richness of its imagery, and the meaning of its theology.

But the congregation questioned me about the size of the ark, its probable landing place, and the difficulty of handling large wild animals. Their questions were not my questions.

In seminary, my friends and I worked with issues such as Central America, disarmament, apartheid, and refugees. In the parish, the conservative constituents preferred issues such as pornography, gambling, drinking, and drug abuse. From our church's point of view, some issues were safe and Christian; others were liberal and purely political.

Many ministers underestimate the ideological suspicion with which congregations greet seminary graduates. New pastors err when they view their task in the first parish as the converting of misguided fundamentalists to the "true way," or the awakening of dulled consciences to crucial social causes. Pastors cannot provoke people into a deeper or broader faith by confrontations on the Virgin birth or by arguments about the authorship of certain Scriptures. Pastors insensitive to ideological differences may alienate or infuriate church members before appropriate time is spent in building a pastoral relationship that can survive theological or political differences.

On the other hand, new pastors err when they discard their own theological training and biblical criticism as being irrelevant to the parish. Pastors who leave behind their learning or disguise their sensitivities to social issues may have difficulty keeping their own faith growing and vital, free from stagnation. They may begin to believe they have compromised their integrity or forsaken their call.

Family Circumstances

Finally, numerous practical circumstances of living make parish ministry different from seminary culture. When I graduated from seminary, I received the first full-time salary in my life, and Esther began her teaching career. We were not rich, but we suddenly fared far better than we had as students. With this change came numerous unforeseen problems. Our jump in salary was accompanied by a larger jump in initial spending habits. We spent our first two years trying to pay the debts incurred during the first three months after graduation.

We also had tremendous trouble adjusting to quarterly tax payments; some were even sent in after the deadline. We needed to purchase furniture to complement the few things that were provided in the parsonage; we needed a second car, since we both worked and kept independent schedules. And unexpectedly large amounts, which I didn't fully comprehend or effectively anticipate, were deducted from my pastor's salary package to support denominational pension and insurance programs. We simply did not know the financial ropes, and there had been no seminary course or denominational program to prepare us for such practical and immediate details.

Since the seminary-to-parish move took us from a large city to a smaller town, job opportunities for my wife were more limited. She found a teaching position, but her work began several months after we arrived, and those early months were nearly unbearable for her. She had left friends, changed jobs, and adopted new roles. She needed emotional support as much as I did, but during the first summer she had no job to bring sustaining personal relationships. By the end of the summer I knew a large number of people, while she knew few; I had work to do that brought focus to my energies and fulfillment to my spirit, but she felt she was floundering with no direction or network of support.

Church members invited her participation, but they tended to derive their expectations from a traditional view of the minister's wife: She was invited to teach Sunday school and help with Bible school and the youth group. These were things Esther had little interest in or enthusiasm for, but she felt bad about turning people down when help was really needed. It was several months before she felt comfortable participating in the life of the church according to her own needs and desire for service, rather than according to the congregation's expectations.

Depending on their age, children can experience the same cultural transitions. They may feel pressured by the expectations of others and the high visibility of the family. They also have moved from relative anonymity to a unique and conspicuous place in the church.

We also discovered that the move from student housing to a parsonage was traumatic. We had no idea how much time and effort it takes to keep a house and lawn in respectable shape. With a second-hand lawn-mower, a few tools, virtually no gardening knowledge and even less enthusiasm, we were expected to keep the parsonage lawn according to the rather high standards set by our neighborhood. The congregation was proud of its property and expected a certain level of respectability, which we had trouble maintaining.

Since Esther and I had attended college and seminary in larger cities, we had forgotten that shopping and entertainment are different in small communities. Many of our most enjoyable evenings in the city had included concerts, museum exhibits, and well-known theatrical productions. We would spend our evenings in used-bookstores or going to discount movies or browsing through the university library. In the city, we seldom had trouble finding fashionable clothes that fit, and we were able to shop for groceries late at night when it suited our schedule. But all that changed when we moved—our entertainment and our shopping habits were forced to conform to the limits set by small-town life.

An endless number of small, day-to-day routines of family life change when we move from seminary to parish. These are less dramatic for graduates who have lived in small-town parsonages as student pastors, or those who take appointments in cities the same size as those where their seminaries were located. But nearly all pastors experience a noticeable and, in some ways, painful change in family routines as they move to the first parish.

Resources for Culture Shock

Culture shock? The term adequately describes the move from seminary to parish. The term also describes every major change we make in ministry. People experience its effects when they move from one career to another, from one form of ministry to another, even from one church to another. We cannot escape the trauma, but we can develop some skills and insights to help make the transitions easier. Culture shock should not be allowed to debilitate our spirits and undermine our purposes. It cannot be avoided, but the way we approach it and cope with it can make it part of our spiritual growth and development.

Seminaries entrust their graduates with very valuable resources. Through years of study, students gain a basically solid and workable theology, and the tools for sound biblical scholarship. They enjoy the experience of living in a sustaining community with brothers and sisters in Christ. Their sensitivity to pressing social and political issues is awakened. Students receive what they need to begin to fulfill their vocation and to realize God's purpose for their lives.

But these resources are not easily accepted by the faithful of the local church or automatically useful in the local congregation. What are newly graduated pastors to do?

Some new pastors may conclude that what they learned in seminary is of little help in the parish. Some stop reading significant theological and biblical literature, cancel their subscriptions to *Sojourners* and *Christian Century,* and soon lose the addresses and phone numbers of their seminary friends.

They may explain this behavior by saying, "Seminary wasn't practical enough, and my theology papers didn't prepare me at all for the parish ministry." Because of the urgency of mastering the work of parish ministry, they may slip into a pragmatic approach to ministry. Their criterion for measuring the good of any resource: "Does it work where I am? Does it help me now?" Certainly these are crucial concerns in the early years of ministry. New pastors, however, may begin to become so focused on the "how to" of ministry that they lose sight of its "what" and "why."

Other graduates encountering culture shock despair over the differences between seminary life and parish ministry, then respond by dividing their world into two parts—their own personal faith, work, and relationships, and the faith, work, and relationships of the local church. They function in ministry as if it were merely a job, while they find their own fulfillment and sustenance in their personal reading and study. They teach *Ten Easy Steps to Successful Prayer* to the local church, while personally sustaining themselves with more substantial spiritual-formation studies. They teach the fundamentals of the Bible to the church, while they prefer more critical methods of study. They value what they have been taught in seminary, but they cannot teach what they value to the local church. Such pastors treat the laity as co-workers, but receive their relational sustenance only from ministerial colleagues. They divide their public life in the local church from their inner life of private theological thinking, silent social activism, and continued peer relationships.

Those ministers who handle culture shock by dividing their world into two parts make little or no attempt to translate the knowledge and experience gained from seminary into the new context of parish life. This leads to a schizophrenic existence that requires a great deal of emotional energy.

New pastors also run the risk of losing self-respect because they are not integrating theology and practice. By failing to do so, they risk losing their vocational integrity, feeling that they know the truth but cannot tell it, or that they see clearly the vision from seminary but can never realize it in the local church. The spirit that sustains them comes from beyond the local church, rather than through its people and mission.

In time, such pastors may grow increasingly cynical about the church and bitter about their place within it. They value their education and are sustained by it, but they can't, for the life of them, put it to work for the purpose for which they have been sent to the local church.

There is another possible response to the problem of what to do with seminary learning in the pastoral setting. Some pastors stay on the "seminary track"; they study and grapple principally with issues raised in seminary courses, without putting energy into the practical issues raised by the local church. This response is not productive and probably does not lead to long or fulfilling pastorates. In fact, such an approach probably will lead to a great deal of anger on the part of both pastor and people.

Finally, there is a more constructive response to culture shock. Some graduates realize that they will never find happiness and integrity in the local church unless they discover some way to translate the experience and knowledge of seminary into the context of congregational life. Only then does seminary education become meaningful and fully useful, serving as the foundation it was intended to be.

Some seminary graduates bring to parish life a sound theology, a sensitive ethic, and the experience of nurturing relationships, and manage to translate these resources into a sustaining vision of ministry for themselves and for the local church. They do not know more than other graduates; in fact, they may seem more willing than the others to admit how much they need to learn. They maintain the inquisitiveness to learn and the determination to grow that helped them through seminary. These pastors experience many of the same setbacks and disappointments as the others, but their vision of the church includes that probability, and their theological and relational resources sustain them through the difficulties.

I have experienced all these alternatives in the face of culture shock. I have acted as if parts of my seminary background are totally irrelevant in the local church, and I have lived the double life of valuing one social issue while promoting another. I have even tried to hide in my study, contenting myself with significant readings, believing that the practical problems outside my door are really irrelevant and hoping they will go away.

But I sincerely believe in the possibility of bringing the best of the seminary experience into parish ministry. My most fulfilling moments were those when I felt faithful to my original vision of ministry and effective in expressing that to the people of the parish. But in order for the learning and experience of seminary to help the minister and the people served, some translating must take place. The structure of academic life must translate into habits of personal discipline, intentional planning, and time management, in the less-structured environment of the parish. The insight gained from interest and activity in social causes must translate into caring ministries that sensitize local churches enough to address the needs of people who hurt, without alienating the people available to help. Seminary's more sophisticated theological and biblical understandings must translate into vital new nourishing images for the local church.

And the new minister cannot discard the seminary network of meaningful relationships, but must exchange it for a new network which includes some of those same friends, some new peers near at hand, and some friends from the local community. The pastor must translate the healthy experiences of those close friendships in seminary into helpful interpersonal skills and insights into how to develop and sustain nurturing relationships in the parish.

Think of all the harsh transitions survived by the apostle Paul. Yet to every new situation he faced, he brought with him the best of his past—his education, his Jewish teaching, his powerful philosophical mind, his Roman sense of law and organization, his relationships with people throughout the Mediterranean. No matter how painful or fulfilling his past, he managed to make use of it in the present. He integrated all he had experienced into every new situation, and that is the secret to healthy transition. Whether leaving one career for another or changing from one church or community to another, take everything with you into the new land. Translate what is useful from the past into helpful resources for the present.

I began this chapter with the culture shock my wife and I experienced when we moved to Great Britain. After some weeks the disorientation and frustration began to ease, and we established sustaining relationships that nourished and strengthened us. We adapted to the changes and adopted new routines. In the end, we were rewarded and enriched beyond measure by the experience of living and learning and working in a new and different environment.

Many things helped us through the cultural adjustments. Guidebooks and British/American dictionaries helped. The kindly advice of Americans who had previously served in England helped. Most important, it helped immensely to share our experiences with other Americans who were feeling the culture shock at the same time.

We had an advantage. We at least had known in our minds that we would be in a different culture in Britain. This is not as easy to perceive when we move through transitions in the ministry. This, however, is precisely the approach we need to take. We move into a new culture. We know that in the transition, we may want to hold on to the old life. We are unsure of the new and will feel uncomfortable at times. It is somewhat similar to what we may have gone through in transitions past. But now we must move on. The issue is not whether we will make the transition, but how well we will make it. There are some things we can do that will help. It is to those suggestions that we will turn in Part II.

Questions for Reflection

Do you remember the disorientation of your move from seminary to parish? What other transitions in your past caused you the most stress? What was the source of the pain?

What do you resent about transitions?

What coping mechanisms helped you through?

What has been the most recent major change in your life? If you have moved recently or changed careers, how is your new role different from your old?

How do your new relationships compare to those from the past?

How has the basis for your self-esteem and sense of accomplishment changed?

What do you miss most about your previous life? Who do you still grieve for?

How has your family experienced the transition? Has the transition changed your family?

If you are in seminary now, what do you anticipate will be the most difficult part of moving to the local church? Are you convinced that certain churches hold no interest for your ministry?

Part Two

Reclaiming Your Call

5

Striving Side by Side

The Grace of Shared Ministry

Aretired army chaplain shared with me the theory behind a soldier's training. Combat soldiers must never feel both powerless and alone at the same time. They may feel one of those emotions, but to experience both at once causes them to lose all ability to function effectively. Feeling powerless *and* alone paralyzes them with fear, causes them to surrender to hopelessness. So the army equips soldiers with a sense of power, teaching them that with proper weapons and expertise, a single soldier can overcome any number of opponents and defend against incredible superiority of arms. And the army places all combat soldiers in teams, companies, squadrons, and crews, surrounded by buddies and in clear communication with supervisors.

A sense of powerlessness *and* isolation can undermine any mission. Pastors, no less than soldiers, wither into painful ineffectiveness if they sever themselves from the spiritual resources that empower them and isolate themselves from the sustaining relationships that enfold them.

Maintaining contact with people who share our vision requires initiative and discipline. Through our covenant with other pastors, we experience the empowering grace

CORRECTION

Robert Schnase is Pastor of First United Methodist Church in McAllen, Texas. Wesley United Methodist Church is found approximately 30 miles away in Harlingen, Texas. The publishers regret the error on the back cover of this book.

Any comments about this book, *Testing and Reclaiming Your Call to Ministry*, may be made directly to the author at the following address:

First United Methodist Church
221 N. Main
P.O. Box 1568
McAllen, Texas 78502

of God, offering us a key resource through which to keep in touch with our call.

A Mentor

The Gift of Experience

In an abundance of counselors there is safety.
                                                                —*Proverbs 11:14*

In *The Odyssey,* when the goddess Athena desired to advise and encourage young Telemachus, floundering in indecision as he awaited Odysseus' return, she took the human form of an older friend, Mentor. According to the story, Mentor advised Telemachus about what steps to take, renewed his courage, restored his vision of purpose, and put a new spirit in him. Telemachus thanked Mentor for his counsel and vowed never to forget it.

Ever since Homer, *mentor* has referred to a trusted advisor who gives invaluable counsel. Business consultants use the word to describe an able older confidant who assists a newcomer into the career world and offers friendly, helpful advice.

Every pastor needs a mentor, a more experienced minister with trustworthy insights and skills. New pastors especially need this guidance, but established pastors also benefit from the counsel of more knowledgeable colleagues.

The mentor relationship helps in a number of ways. First, an experienced pastor has the advantage of hindsight and the perspective of time. He or she can see more clearly the significance of various tasks and skills and can help put both the victories and defeats in proper perspective. When ministers encounter conflicts with church members or feel the full weight of congregational intransigence, they need someone to help them sort through the troubles. Someone who has personally survived such times offers the sincerest sympathy and the most trustworthy hope. Without this critical relationship, pastors interpret every criticism from the congregation as failure and every setback as absolute defeat. Only the perspective of time teaches that defeat is temporary and that feelings of failure are natural.

Second, the veteran pastor offers a wealth of practical information. Newer pastors often do not even know the right questions to ask. They don't know what they need to know. As they approach their first wedding or prepare for their first funeral, they need someone who can offer helpful hints without making them feel dumb for not knowing what to do. Mentors guide neophytes through the maze of denominational reports and help them complete the myriad of official forms. Seminary studies offer little help with such practical matters, and few books offer the wisdom that comes with experience. Questions will arise about church administration and personnel that only someone who has walked the same road can fully answer.

Third, the mentor helps the less accomplished pastor discern the important from the trivial. All new pastors need help in setting priorities and defining objectives. Every church will receive hundreds of requests for special offerings each year, and each minister will receive countless invitations to important meetings. The newcomer needs to hear the voice of experience decide which offerings really matter and which meetings really require one's full attention. New ministers need someone with whom to test new ideas and try out new plans before actually putting them into practice in the local church. No one needs to learn everything by the painful method of trial and error. The new pastor can profit from the experience of others.

Fourth, the mentor gives insight into the *informal* networks of influence and authority in the denominational structure. In seminary, students learn about *formal* denominational structures—which officials make certain decisions and who sets policy and how appointments are made. They learn the way agencies of the denomination work and how one committee relates to another. Although valuable, that knowledge does not fully describe the way things happen in practice. Certain leaders have an inordinate effect upon what gets done, regardless of what office they hold; other pastors hold important positions but really cannot make things happen effectively. Also, some policies are strictly adhered to and uniformly enforced, while others are of little consequence. A mentor can help answer many of these questions: Who gets things done? Who really holds the power? What goes on behind the scenes? Only ministers with accumulated knowledge can give insight into the subtleties of denominational authority and offer perspectives on the people who hold positions of leadership. They can introduce their newer colleagues to other leaders and advise them about how to work effectively on denominational committees. All this information comes only from those who have watched the system work over a number of years.

Finally, the mentor encourages the newer pastor. The Bible says that Paul often took time to encourage younger churches and their leaders as he traveled. *Encouragement* literally means "to put courage into." Ministers need that today as much as they did two thousand years ago. Mentors cheer new ministers through their victories and reassure them when things do not go well. They stimulate and reward creative responses and offer heartening hope when things seem dismal. They prompt personal and professional growth and keep alive the vision of ministry when all appears dim. They help pastors through the times of testing and explore the meaning of the call from a more mature perspective. The mentor's friendly voice comforts and sustains, challenges and counsels. Mentors listen, teach, and share their own hurts and sorrows. But most of all, they encourage.

Of course, it is one thing to describe the ideal mentor and another to find one! I recommend someone who has at least fifteen years more experience in ministry than you. The perspective of a pastor who has only three or four years more experience may not differ significantly from your own. On the other hand, if a pastor retired from the ministry five or more years ago, you may value the long-range perspective, but his or her practical understanding of procedures could be outdated. Choose someone old enough to have a wealth of experience but young enough to be relevant to you and your ministry.

Seek someone whose ministry you respect. More important than the size church your mentor serves is his or her integrity and approach to ministry. Choose someone you judge to be competent and to have integrity, someone whose insight you can trust and who will honor confidentiality. Select a person who is still growing and learning.

Look for someone who can give you time when you need it. If your mentor lives too far away or never has time to meet with you, then you may not have access to counsel when you need it most.

Look for someone who will share negative experiences as well as positive, who will express unhappy emotions as well as joyful. You want a person who is honest, not artificial. Don't choose a minister who only boasts and has no recall of setbacks or failure. Seek someone with a well-balanced ministry, a pastor who has appropriately met the challenges of God's call.

Look for a minister whose quality and style of leadership you admire. Consider your own need for growth. Where do you need help? If you're facing a financial nightmare in your new church, choose someone with the administrative expertise you lack. If you are recently divorced, seek one who has come through similar grief in a healthy and effective manner.

Finally, find someone who wants to help you learn and grow. Your mentor's willingness and enthusiasm should match your delight in working with him or her. Obviously, you will be discouraged by someone who would really rather not bother with inexperienced pastors.

You cannot find the perfect minister. There are none. The qualities I have described fit most of the ministers you will come to know in your career. You can find integrity, trustworthiness, and leadership in ministers serving small, medium, and large churches across your denomination. The mentor relationship, however, has a special chemistry, and not every pastor who could serve as mentor is necessarily the best prospect for you. You must decide who can fill that role and then take the initiative to create the relationship.

If you are an associate pastor, find someone other than your senior pastor to be your mentor. You will learn about ministry from your senior pastor through working together and sharing, but it is almost impossible for anyone to serve as both boss and mentor. The roles are different and one sometimes will conflict with the other. You need the perspective of an outsider, who can help you see your way through staff difficulties in a more effective and less threatening manner than can your own senior pastor.

You may make the relationship with your mentor as formal or as informal as you like. If you have a friend close by who fits the description, an informal relationship might work best. Ask for a lunch appointment. Get into the habit of visiting together about once a month. Your meetings may include chit-chat and serious questions; the topics may meander from family to church to career. Enjoy your lunches, but just because they are informal does not mean they are unimportant. Take with you a list of specific questions about things going on in your church. Share the successes and the defeats as you experience them. And let your friend know how much these meetings mean to you and how much you learn from them.

When I began my ministry, one of my closest friends was a minister about twenty-five years older who served a church forty miles away. We'd meet for lunch and talk about everything under the sun; no matter was too insignificant or too important. Our visits were friendly, and I enjoyed his support and interest in my ministry. I also called him fairly frequently to ask him his advice about many things—how to complete statistical reports or how to hire a church janitor. But most important, I received guidance about handling my own inner conflicts, depressions, and aspirations. I never called my friend a mentor; he was just a friend. We never formally agreed to meet and never established an agenda for our meetings, but our relationship fulfilled the definition of mentorship.

A more formal relationship works best for many people. This would require a written agreement about how frequently you and your mentor will meet and what issues you will take up; prepare a calendar of meetings and discussion topics, including some readings for yourself as part of the learning contract. Take time to evaluate your progress as the year goes along.

Soon out of seminary, I served a church with tremendous financial difficulties in the same town where another minister, highly gifted in church administration, served a larger church. I contracted to meet with him ten times for two-hour sessions to discuss church administration and finance. In preparation for each session, I read various resources and came prepared with a long list of questions. We focused on functional skills, but we also talked at length about defeats and victories, and the ensuing pain or satisfaction. You can establish contracts on topics such as administration, evangelism, or preaching, or on relational subjects like family life, conflict management, risk-taking, or handling criticism. A formal learning contract requires clarity about what you want or need to learn.

Your denomination may require you to develop a learning contract with a supervisory pastor as part of its ministerial training, or as a probationary requirement, and here a word of caution may apply. If the pastor assigned to you must decide on your qualifications or offer an evaluation of your progress to an examining board, this person may be helpful to you, but not as a mentor. For the same reason the senior pastor cannot serve as both boss and mentor, another pastor cannot serve as both examiner and confidant. Sharing in an atmosphere of complete trust is essential for learning from your mentor, and such trust seldom develops in an atmosphere of evaluation and examination.

In addition to the formal and informal models for mentorship, short-term learning experiences can be invaluable. If you know of a highly talented minister who lives too far away to meet with regularly, consider asking if you could meet a few times during a visit to that community. For instance, if you admire the preaching ability of a particular minister and know that she can offer constructive evaluations of your own preaching, perhaps you could contract with her to meet with you two hours a day for three days in a row, to listen to your preaching and offer her insights. This model best suits those who wish to acquire specific skills from someone highly gifted in that area. Make plans far in the future so that you are not an encumbrance to your mentor's busy schedule.

But find a mentor! Seek a formal or an informal model, or both, for mentorship. Take the responsibility for initiating the relationship. A good mentor is one of your most valuable resources for growth in ministry, and most experienced ministers will feel privileged that you have asked for help. They will enjoy your relationship as much as you do, and they will learn in the process. Do not hesitate to ask.

In the absence of such counsel, it's easy to feel devastated by the inevitable conflicts and temporary setbacks. To discover that others have walked the same path, have survived the time of testing, and even have triumphed over such adversities, is counsel worth any price. It can be yours, if you take the initiative.

The Covenant of Ministers

The Only Ones Who Understand

And he called to him the twelve, and began to send them out two by two. —Mark 6:7

Why do you suppose Jesus sent out the disciples two by two? Perhaps he knew the resistance they would encounter and the struggles they would experience. He knew they would need each other's strength and encouragement. Nothing is so desperate as a lonely struggle.

The relationship pastors share with other pastors remains critical for keeping the call in focus. Most ordained ministers sense intuitively their need for other clergy, but unless this need is intentionally pursued, such spirit-sustaining relationships do not develop.

Pastors need others who understand the unique relationship they have with their churches. They need others with whom they can discuss freely the trouble spots and troubling people in their ministry. They need to know that other pastors experience the same things.

No doctor would let a situation become critical without testing an evaluation with associates, colleagues, or specialists. Some kinds of advice and insight come only from peers.

Ministers need people with whom we can laugh about the humorous situations we create, people with whom we can cry about our bitter disappointments. Clergy friends provide these needs without jeopardizing pastors' relationship with their church members.

Other clergy offer a forum for pastors to share our deepest theological doubts, to listen to one another's complaints about the church without taking offense. Pastors need a place where we can step away temporarily from our role of caregivers to experience the grace of being care receivers.

Many clergy—city pastors as well as those who work in remote rural communities—experience tremendous loneliness. We need some way to break through that isolation. We just need friends.

It's not that friends can't be found in our own congregations. It's that pastors need people who understand through first-hand experience what we are going through. Jesus sent out his disciples two by two because he knew they needed each other if they were going to fulfill the tasks of discipleship.

Many pastors establish their most enduring friend-ships with other clergy. When pastors leave a congrega-tion, they may have difficulty maintaining ties to their lay friends without infringing on succeeding pastors, but friendships with other pastors survive many moves through the years.

When ministers submit to ordination, they enter into covenant—not just with God, but with other ministers who have responded to the same lifelong vocation. And with covenant comes mutual obligation and commit-ment. Ministers take responsibility for encouraging one another in love, and they hold one another accountable in mutual trust and concern. Pastors not only are responsible to their local congregations but to one another for upbuilding the Body of Christ.

When I visit with another minister, I experience our time together as a short rest stop during a long hike. We lay down our burdens for awhile, enjoy the respite, and then take up our packs to continue, discovering that because of the break, the mile ahead is a little easier than the last. I feel refreshed, more in touch with my profession and my calling. The short interlude reminds me of the mysterious work we do; it helps me see my small part in a much larger movement. We may talk shop during most of the visit, but something more significant takes place. We both leave a little more confident that despite the rocky ground and ravenous birds in our own fields, the Kingdom's yield will indeed bring forth a hundredfold.

Seek out the pastors in your area for fellowship or study. Get to know pastors of your own denomination and also those of other denominations. Their perspectives may differ from your own, but their experiences in ministry are similar.

Start by simply inviting another pastor to lunch. If you don't know the person, it may seem awkward at first, but keep at it. Seldom do friendships deepen to their richest levels during first encounters.

Sometimes informal social gatherings are most enjoyable. Consider having a regular gathering for supper, inviting all the pastors in your area—young and old, known to you and new to you. You do not need to hold any position of authority to host such a gathering; others will appreciate the opportunity as much as you. Include the families. Spouses and children need contact with others who are going through the same things they are.

Many pastors would enjoy weekly lectionary studies, Bible studies, or book reviews; they may feel more comfortable in task-oriented groups than at social gatherings. If every pastor wishes to study something different, don't let the differences keep you from gathering, because the deeper purposes of the companionship will transcend whatever you choose to study. You are developing a support network as well as enhancing your knowledge of a study topic.

With a task-oriented group, don't let strict commitment to the agenda keep you from listening to one another's personal victories and defeats. If someone needs support, adjust your discussion. Do not ignore the pain. The study may be the occasion for the gathering, but sometimes the group will fulfill quite a different purpose. When someone shares a significant joy or sorrow from his or her personal life or ministry, listen. Offer encouragement.

Some pastors gather in more formally contracted groups with a trained leader. I once participated in a group that met once each month with a skilled counselor. Eight pastors who attended regularly helped pay the professional fee. We observed strict confidentiality, and none of us went through the year without appreciating the group as a significant help during a time of need.

Such enriching and regular contact with other ministers does not happen automatically. For your own good, and in obedience to your ordination covenant with other ministers, take the initiative. You will find yourself sustained, and you will offer a tremendous ministry to the other pastors.

You could begin with a letter to other clergy in the area about an initial gathering, following the letter with a phone call to answer questions. When you meet, let the group decide the focus, content, and regular meeting time. Establish the level of commitment. Will this be "come when you can," or will it require a more significant commitment to attendance? If a group meeting cannot be worked out to everyone's satisfaction, you are no worse off. Then you must take the initiative to meet with pastors individually—for lunch or recreation or study— as your way of fulfilling this important need.

Invite people, but don't push. Evoke their desire for shared ministry; don't coerce them to come to a meeting by making them feel guilty. And seldom can supervisors establish good support groups; the presence of pastors who have authority over other pastors generally changes the nature of the group.

Remember that the purpose is "to encourage and build one another up" (I Thess. 5:11). Avoid competition. If a meeting serves only as a forum for comparing salaries, spreading rumors, or boasting, it will create discouragement. No one leaves a discussion about salaries feeling better; the fruit of such comparison is envy, vexation, ambition, strife. Such gatherings cause us to lose the focus of our call. Our time together is to encourage one another in Christ.

Paul knew the joy of "striving side by side for the faith" with our brothers and sisters in ministry. To fulfill God's call, we need one another. It is hard to be faithful alone, so don't wait until you desperately need support to form a regular gathering of ministers. Presume that you already need it, even if no crisis is impending. Work on the foundations of your ministry when the weather is fair. In the teeth of the storm, fortification is difficult.

Questions for Reflection

List the five most influential pastors in your formative years of ministry. What did each one most distinctively contribute to your understanding of ministry? What advice or encouragement has most influenced your ministry? What advice would you give to someone considering God's call to ordained ministry?

Who are your most intimate friends in ministry? Who have you learned most from? To whom have you turned for help recently? Who turns to you?

List the five pastors in your life today who most deeply influence your own sense of ministry? Do you have regular contact with any of them? What do you respect about their ministry? How can you more intentionally strengthen your relationships?

What are the implications of your ordination covenant on your relationship with other pastors? Do you sense any mutual obligation or responsibility? How do you fulfill those obligations?

How do you feel after you meet with a group of pastors? What other pastors know your deepest aspirations? Your deepest fears? Who are your most intimate and supportive companions in your spiritual life? How can you strengthen those relationships?

6

Pressing on Toward the Goal

The Grace of Disciplined Learning

Everyone who flies has heard the speech. The flight attendant dangles the oxygen mask from the overhead compartment to simulate an emergency, and then shows how to place it over your face by pulling the rubber straps over your head.

When I first heard those instructions, the flight attendant added, "If you are traveling with a young child, first place a mask over your own face before you do the same for the child." This troubled me. How could parents think of themselves first!

But with a moment's thought, I realized the common sense and profound truth of the instructions. If I do not have oxygen, I cannot help the child. If I do not fulfill my own fundamental needs, I have absolutely nothing to offer anyone else. To care for anyone else, I must first care for myself.

We cannot offer Christ's living water without occasionally pausing at the well to taste it ourselves. We need regular and disciplined ways to replenish our spirits and refill the empty places in our own souls, before we can hope to refresh others with God's gracious love.

Private Devotions

A Special Time and Place

"What must we do, to be doing the works of God?" Jesus answered them, "This is the work of God, that you believe in him whom he has sent." —*John 6:28-29*

We hear so much about visitation, evangelism, preaching, and leadership that we believe a pastor's usefulness derives solely from performance in those skills. Frequently, however, a pastor's effectiveness depends on what happens in the quiet times with God. Before presenting any idea to a church committee, before any visitation, before any sermon, before taking any leadership initiative, the pastor needs time for reflection and prayer, to consider whether the proposed action has the sanction of God and is consistent with the will of God, as best the pastor can discern it. In matters of ethical choice, we serve a constituency of one. Pastors need time to measure a proposed activity against a wisdom higher than our own. To do the works of God, Jesus said, requires that we believe in the One God has sent. Many of the struggles pastors face are not church problems, but problems of our own closeness to God.

In prayer, we consider closely whose will we follow, whose method we choose, whose path we seek. We stay in touch with the most basic of Christian motivations, and in so doing, we stay in touch with our call.

Set aside a time for personal devotions. Don't do it just when you happen to have time, for there will never be time left over from your work. You must make time. Consider it vital, because it is the foundation upon which we build everything else we do. Taking such a discipline seriously can be our hardest work but the most productive times of our ministry.

In recent years, there has been a new emphasis in most major denominations on spiritual formation. Pastors have discovered something missing from their spiritual lives, and that missing something is not peripheral, but central. Pastors are attending prayer retreats and spiritual-formation seminars.

Any relationship needs communication. Imagine two people who live together but never speak to each other. Despite their physical proximity, can you really say they have any kind of relationship? You can begin to understand someone's heart and mind only through regular dialogue. Our relationship with God requires the same kind of regular communication, especially since we presume to present God's Word to others.

When pastors lose touch with their devotional life, they tend to blame outside circumstances for their dissatisfactions. They think that if only they received more recognition, or a larger salary, or a bigger church, then things would go well and they would find satisfaction. But without a solid spiritual life, they only take their hunger with them to the next church. The first essential step toward dealing with external troubles is to settle our internal disturbances and resolve our inner conflicts.

Precisely because we work in an occupation that serves people, we need time alone away from people to help us rekindle our compassion. If Jesus needed time away from the crowds for prayer, what makes us presume that we can work tirelessly without it?

Set aside a regular period of time to open your heart and mind to Scripture, or meditate on prayers or readings from a directed devotional book. Don't be afraid if your mind wanders. Daydreaming helps keep our imaginations alive; it helps us picture the positive outcomes toward which we strive.

While visiting with a pastor well-known for her fine exegesis and excellent preaching, I asked if she ever preached from the psalms. She answered that the psalms speak to her so personally and profoundly that she cannot separate herself from them enough to preach from them.

Her personal love of the psalms, feeding her soul and nourishing her spirit, stood in sharp contrast to my narrow utilitarian use of Scripture as the source for preaching and guide for teaching. She used Scripture and prayer personally; I tended to use them professionally. I realized then my need to take my own spiritual life more seriously.

Some people pray best while surrounded by silence. Others immerse themselves in fine music. Still others need to be nurtured by nature. Some pray best at home; others at church; some in a rocker; some while walking. Your devotional time should make you feel renewed and strengthened, better centered and recommitted to action. Like returning to physical exercise after long neglect, sometimes the first sessions seem strained and unhelpful. It takes time to develop the skills to make your time meaningful and helpful. Don't expect too much too soon.

Sabbath is the time to focus all that you have and all that you are on the One who created you. How ironic that we pastors are the most likely to neglect the sabbath. For the pastor, Sunday is a day of work. So when is your sabbath?

Use a special time and place. Protect it like a precious treasure. You will discover that the time enhances all your hours, and the place moves with you throughout the day.

The Pastor's Study

Learning to Read Again

Take heed to yourself and to your teaching; hold to that, for by so doing you will save both yourself and your hearers.
—I Timothy 4:16

Pastors usually have an office at the church where they meet the public, conduct business, counsel parishioners, and administer the affairs of the church. But pastors also need an inner sanctum for reading and writing, for concentration and reflection, away from the traffic of the church office. The pastor needs a study.

More than a place, the pastor's study describes an arena of work as vital as pastoral care, preaching, and administration. To grow in understanding and effectiveness requires study.

Personal study frequently lacks focus, depth, and concentration for exploring an area of ministry. We dabble here and there, first in one area and then another, instead of taking a thorough look at a topic or developing any mastery of a subject. If we do not constantly revive our motivation toward intellectual pursuits, lethargy slides us downward from studying books to reading journals, to leafing through magazines, to perusing newspapers, and finally to watching sit-coms on television. Intellectual inertia bogs us down. The path of least effort leads to spiritual quiescence.

Sometimes with a quick glance at the books in the study, one can tell when a minister graduated from seminary. It's sad to see nothing newer than those required in the senior year.

Just as someone on a junk-food diet needs to learn how

to eat again, when the pastor's study habits lose fervor and focus, it's time to learn to read again.

Take every opportunity to read. The more I read, the more easily my teaching plans flow. Even when I read things unrelated to theology, I find that my sermon writing moves more smoothly. Study keeps the creative juices flowing. Our minds need something streaming in before anything can flow out.

Reading provides the opportunity to personally visit with the great thinkers of the ages. Imagine hosting fine theologians and great storytellers in your living room! What would you ask if the world's leading counselor sat before you in your study? View books as companions in your intellectual and spiritual journey.

Read for balance and thoroughness. Our hunger to address immediate needs causes us to reach first for the how-to books, which abound on the practice of ministry. Use them wisely and they will help you, but balance your appetite with a taste for the foundational, the bedrock theological and philosophical works that challenge assumptions and deepen understanding.

For example, there are many how-to books on evangelism. Read them and apply their practices, but also study the great theologians to understand more deeply the "why" of evangelism, the place of Christ, the power of sin, and the purpose of the church. Knowing "how to" fixes immediate problems; knowing "why" gives a vision of the church toward which we can strive for the long haul. Balance the fast food with some well-rounded meals. And occasionally, taste some fine cuisine.

Read nontheological work as avidly as religious studies. Some of the best insight into the human soul comes from fiction and poetry; excellent perceptions into our community life come from sociology, psychology, and economics.

And read for fun as well as for work. Whatever form your ministry takes, our principal job is to deliver the most important message in the world. Regular reading helps both our public speaking and our personal sharing. It helps us to articulate thoughts accurately, enriches vocabulary, and increases dexterity with the tools of language.

Take opportunities to "book up" on special subjects. Accept invitations to teach subjects with which you're unfamiliar, then study for the occasion. Such assignments stretch us.

Make a place to study. If the office is too busy, find another room in the church, use an extra bedroom at the parsonage, or lay claim to a study cubicle at a nearby library. Pastors need a place with their most-used resources close at hand and their writing tools ready to go.

Make time for reading. The average adult American spends between thirty and forty hours a week watching television. You say this statistic doesn't apply to you? For a couple of weeks, keep track of the number of hours you spend watching television and the number of hours you read. If you seriously want to redeem some time for reading, the solution is obvious.

Consider joining a reading group, either with other pastors or with church members. It's easier to let yourself down than to disappoint others, and a mutual covenant strengthens resolve.

When we are widely read, we can better understand the deeper motivations for our work by keeping in touch with the great ideas, the highest aspirations, the deepest insights into human life. John Wesley told his preachers, "Develop a taste for reading or else return to your trade."

All the great church founders knew the vital importance of a literate, well-read clergy, in touch with the world, aware of its philosophies, and knowledgeable and skilled in theology.

Don't feel embarrassed if you are found reading on the job. It's a task the church requires of you in order to fulfill your vocation effectively.

Continuing Education

Broadening Horizons and Sharpening Skills

Do not be conformed to this world but be transformed by the renewal of your mind. —Romans 12:2

Would you want to be treated by a surgeon who hadn't cracked a book or read a journal in five years? Would you hire an accountant who hadn't studied tax law for ten years?

All professionals need continuing education. God may be the same yesterday, today, and tomorrow, but we live in a rapidly changing world. Our ways of understanding God have developed; new methods of teaching the Bible have become available; each generation faces challenges that require new counseling skills. For effectiveness and relevance, renewing the pastoral mind is a lifelong task.

And pastors change. Perhaps we felt confident that we knew how to handle some things when we graduated from seminary; but now our experience has expanded, and we are bumping up against new frontiers. We may feel now that we need to know things that back then, we didn't even know we lacked.

We should develop our continuing education according to what we need, rather than according to what's offered. Take the initiative to find or create the course of study you need. Many pastors don't like the alumni lectures at their seminary. But do we stop eating altogether because our usual lunch spot changes chefs? We either adjust our appetite or eat somewhere else, but we eat. Lack of interest in one form of continuing education shouldn't keep you from exploring other alternatives.

Be clear about your purpose for attending educational events. Many folks attend more for reunion than for study. They take no notes, ask few questions, and spend more time visiting in the hallways than listening to the lectures. If you attend for companionship, include study somewhere else in your schedule during the year.

Choose study that requires work. Sometimes we just sit and take notes which we never rework and apply. Do something that requires you to write or speak or practice or discuss.

Submit yourself to someone else's guidance and evaluation. All effective continuing education requires an openness to outside control and feedback. Allow someone else to tell you what to read and write, then invite evaluation.

Consider the full range of continuing education options. A seminary lecture series addresses a large number of people, using well-known leaders. This offers the opportunity to hear these speakers at low cost, while enjoying the companionship of other pastors.

Many pastors prefer workshops that focus on practical skills such as preaching, counseling, or church growth.

Some prefer education that earns credit toward a degree. A good doctorate-of-ministry program integrates theology and practical experience that focuses on a specific area of ministry. Degree programs offer the most highly structured approach to continuing education, but they involve long-term commitment and often considerable expense. Before you enroll, decide whether you are pursing the education or the degree.

One of the best ways to obtain continuing education is to contract personally with a seminary professor or other specialist for supervised work in a particular area of ministry. The contract might call for three or four sessions with the professor, with study assignments in-between. Many pastors overlook such tailor-made programs under expert tutelage. For the cost of their own travel and an honorarium for the teacher, pastors can receive help specific to their own needs. Many seminaries offer independent study programs, allowing pastors to stay at reduced cost while pursuing a project under the guidance of a faculty member.

Reflect on which format suits you best. Do you work better in groups or one-on-one? Do you like lectures, or prefer personal contact?

Consider using fellow pastors for continuing education. You could be surrounded by experts! Within thirty miles of my first pastorate, I discovered pastors with special expertise in evangelism, race relations, work with refugees, and church finance. Arrange for personal tutelage by contracting for a few meetings over a period of time. Your time together will help both of you, but read and prepare before you go. You will appreciate a teacher's insight more if you have already "booked-up" on the subject.

But continuing education is not vacation time. Pastors who do their continuing education on vacation are more likely to skip lectures and take tours instead of settling down to study and learning.

Use the funds your church offers for continuing

education. View it as a legitimate expense of the church to increase your effectiveness as pastor. Communicate to the church clearly how you spend the money and time.

Do something that stretches you. Step beyond the familiar into new terrain. Or if you study in an area in which you already have expertise, see that you move to new frontiers. The point of continuing education is to broaden horizons and sharpen skills.

The key to effective continuing education is the pastor's initiative. Develop a plan with a focus and direction that grows out of your professional needs, which gives strength to a particular area of competence and balance to your overall ministry.

Relational Skills

Making Up for Seminary

And try to learn what is pleasing to the Lord.
　　　　　　　　　　　　　　　　—Ephesians 5:10

One of my friends says that seminaries prepare ministers for everything but the parish. He claims that ministerial education is like a school that trains dentists who will never see anything but in-grown toenails. We learn the wrong skills for daily work in the parish.

For instance, in what percentage of your time in the parish do you use Greek? On the other hand, how frequently do you lead small groups; how often do you face conflict? Yet many seminary graduates have three semesters of Greek and no courses on group dynamics or conflict management.

Seminaries need not provide all these things. They lay a solid theological foundation and offer a framework for ethical thinking and the tools for ongoing study. I don't regret my Greek study, nor do I suggest that core theology be replaced with the practice of ministry. But there is no doubt that many important skills for ministry will need to be acquired by you.

Seminary has not taught a tenth of what you need in the parish. If you approach your work with that in mind, you'll get along much better. A key survival tactic in the parish is humility enough to admit that you don't know everything. Bring with you a curiosity, a desire to learn more, and a willingness to seek constant improvement.

Seminaries teach academic subjects; in the parish, we need practical skills. Seminaries reward theological competence and intellectual proficiency; churches require excellent relational skills as well. Seminaries evaluate individual work; a pastor's effectiveness depends upon working cooperatively with people.

Following is an incomplete list of skills a pastor needs daily, but which few pastors have studied in seminary:

Leadership:

Pastors, willingly or unwillingly, are leaders of people. They need to study leadership and learn their own style of influencing others.

Small-Group Dynamics:

Most of pastors' contact with people is through worship, committee meetings, Bible studies, men's and women's groups. Pastors need to sharpen small-group skills through study in group dynamics. You may wish to contract with a speech therapist or attend speech workshops to increase your effectiveness in speaking.

Management:

Whether pastors manage only volunteers or oversee a large office staff, their effectiveness and happiness depends upon their ability to manage personnel. Personnel management courses and seminars on training and nurturing volunteers offer help.

Conflict:

Nothing depletes strength more than conflict and misunderstanding. Consider attending a seminar in conflict management to learn about temperament types and how they affect your perceptions and appreciation of people. Pastors need quality listening skills, which seldom develop without intentional study and practice.

Aging:

In many congregations, 70 percent of the members are retired. A congregation often evaluates its pastor on the quality of concern shown the homebound and elderly. Younger pastors might attend workshops in gerontology to better understand the experience of older adults.

Power:

Pastors need insight into power dynamics, church finance, and the principles that make for positive change and growth in congregations.

Stress Management:

In addition to sharpening professional abilities, pastors need to develop personal and family skills.

Seminars that help with transitions from one parish to another and workshops that deal with anger and stress are important. Many pastors study ways to overcome procrastination and handle depression. Some seminars help enrich our marriages or deal with sexual issues in parish life.

Learning any of these things pleases the Lord by helping us serve more effectively and compassionately. Few are emphasized in seminary, but many denominational publishing houses address precisely these sorts of issues through their books. General bookstores offer top quality material on stress, procrastination, and depression. The Alban Institute in Washington, D.C., offers courses and there are many university short-term courses or seminars.

The initiative is always yours. Take it. Find out how you can further the education your seminary began. Your education for ministry, if properly perceived, is lifelong. The day you think you know it all is the day your spiritual and professional growth ends.

Journal Keeping

Write to the Heart

Examine yourselves, to see whether you are holding to your faith. Test yourselves. —II Corinthians 13:5

Many times I have no idea how I feel about something until I express myself in words. Talking it out or writing it down gives structure to my thoughts, a perspective to what's going on inside me. A helpful way to sort through experiences is to keep a journal.

The well-kept journal is a photo album of our spiritual travels. It helps us remember where we have been and what we saw and experienced along the way. Often when we face trying times, we forget that we have trod this path before. A journal reminds us of spiritual reserves that we sometimes forget.

When I visit my hometown and see my childhood house, I am amazed at how small it is, compared with its size in my memory. Time changes perceptions. The same thing happens when I try to recall my spiritual ups and downs. The only way to accurately capture the present for future reference is through a regular discipline of recorded experiences. Journals help us test perceptions, ideas, emotions, actions; they help us examine our spirits honestly and freshly.

Don't go to any expense. A ledger book from any variety store works well. You don't need to write well or spell perfectly. You're the only one who will see your work. The purpose of this journal is not to impress.

Write about what you do, but also about how you feel and what you think about what you do. Consider common experiences and reflect on how they fit into your larger aspirations. Write about the positive and also the negative. But don't just write about your troubles—write your way *out* of your troubles.

Set no minimum or maximum for your daily contribution, but write regularly, never letting more than a day or two go by. Even with a short lapse between experience and record, we miss the true feeling.

Why do you suppose sea captains of days past kept such detailed journals? For some reason, knowing where you have been is as important as knowing where you are going. Keeping a record is one of the best ways to stay on course.

Questions for Reflection

What is your greatest source of spiritual renewal? Through what means do you receive the Spirit's guidance?

What prayers, Scriptures, authors, give you the most strength during times of spiritual depletion?

How much time do you spend weekly nourishing your own spiritual life? What is most helpful? What is least helpful?

What's the difference between a professional prayer and a personal prayer?

Is there a difference between Bible study to prepare for a sermon and Bible study to prepare one's soul? Which do you do most?

When you picture yourself five years from now, what additional skills would you like to have? What would you like to be able to do well or understand better?

What do you have planned during the months ahead that will help you achieve those goals?

What relational skills would increase your effectiveness?

How do you hold yourself accountable for your studies? With whom do you share your intellectual pursuits?

What areas have you "booked-up" on recently? On what basis do you choose the books you read?

How much writing do you do? What is the place of writing in your spiritual life?

7

Enjoying Time
Away

Grace from Beyond the Workplace

Who are you when you are not the pastor?
Removed from your ministry and introduced
without your title, what describes your commitments and priorities? Are your nonworking hours
defined just by the absence of work? Or are they filled
with other interests?

A rich and varied private life enhances our professional life and helps us enjoy it more. By developing
outside interests, we can more easily keep our ministry in
perspective; we are less likely to experience minor
tremors as major earthquakes.

Family Time

No Justification Required

---

*If any one does not provide for his relatives, and especially for
his own family, he has disowned the faith and is worse than an
unbeliever.* —*I Timothy 5:8*

Family time, community interests, and recreation
bring blessings immeasurable. Time away from the
church replenishes our spirits, offers balance to ministry,
and helps us remain faithful to God's call without
burning out.

The late Carlyle Marney shocked pastors by beginning his renewal retreats with the question, "How many of you have been unfaithful to your spouse?" After an awkward silence, Marney would go on to explain that marital unfaithfulness takes many forms, that infidelity is a matter of degrees. Ministerial unfaithfulness refers to the tendency to give the highest commitment, deepest love, and greatest time to the church while neglecting our spouses, making our spouses feel second best. Thus many spouses view the energy and time pastors pour into the church through the eyes of jealous, neglected lovers.

Answering God's call to Christian ministry is no virtue if it requires neglecting God's instruction that we should love our family. All professionals feel the stress of balancing familial and career responsibilities. The unusual risk for ministers is that they may justify immense periods of time away from family as God's will and rationalize their neglect as faithfulness to God's call.

At ordination, we publicly express our response to God's call to ministry. At our weddings we express our response to God's call to married life. The same God calls us to both possibilities for service and love. For the married, fulfilling the responsibilities of marriage is part of God's call. It is inconceivable that God would call us to neglect our families. Distance from our families inevitably leads to vocational distress.

Family responsibilities for unmarried pastors may take different forms, but are no less important. Whether directed toward parents and siblings or toward intimate friends, these primary relationships enhance our sense of self-worth and confidence and offer life-supporting emotional sustenance. The security that comes from our most intimate friendships helps us through life crises and through the maze of ministry. Give time to carefully nurture and fortify those precious relationships—for the sake of your loved ones, and for your own sake.

No human love is greater than that shared with our families. We dare not rob each other of this most precious grace, nor can we allow the church to rob us. You need no justification for spending time with your family.

Because you work on Sundays, your days off may not coincide with those of the working world, so if you have children, don't feel embarrassed when seen with them at the park on Tuesday afternoon. People will understand, because their own families are important to them. Or they will learn something from your witness. In either case, feel no need to apologize.

Workaholic parents can destroy the fabric of their home life. Our broken world needs no more models of parents who strive only for personal success and material gain. It needs models of ordinary parents who balance their professional commitments in ways that preserve the family. You will influence your church members positively by protecting your family time.

I don't mean that the purpose of loving your family is to witness to others. You love your family members because they need you and you need them. Luxuriate in the blessings of family life. Accept and enjoy your time with spouse, children, parents.

But families do not stay together without effort. Those of you who are married must realize that marriage requires ongoing maintenance and constant attention. You chose your spouse and committed yourself in total love. To remain faithful you must continually choose and rechoose your spouse in visible and sustaining ways that leave no doubt about your commitment. Therefore you must sometimes choose to spend time with him or her instead of at work.

Most wives and husbands of pastors want to know what's going on. They want to offer support and encouragement. They want respect for their own careers and freedom to choose their own church involvement. They want some sign of interest about their own day-to-day work and consideration for their own aspirations.

Pastors tend to take their jobs home with them, and often a spouse hears only the things that go wrong and the unresolved troubles. This is unfair. Share the positive stories, the quaint incidents, the satisfying conversations. Let your spouse know the experiences that sustain you.

But more dangerous than taking the job home is taking the pastoral role home. A pastor's spouse needs a husband or wife in the evening, not a pastor. Don't try to pastor your own family—spouse, children, parents, or siblings. Sharpen up your counseling skills elsewhere. Nothing kills an intimate conversation like the language of clinical pastoral education.

Plan definite time for your family, and take those dates as seriously as any other appointments. If your church member suggests a meeting for Thursday evening, and you already have another engagement that night, you have no trouble requesting an alternative time. People respect calendar conflicts. Put family time on your calendar and let your sense of previous obligation rule. Simply say that date is taken; no further justification is required. You have no reason to feel guilty about time with your family.

When you leave the job, really leave it. This is difficult to do, especially since you are constantly on call. But you need a time away from the church and its people. Don't count as family time any event that puts you in contact with the church. You and your spouse or children may enjoy a Sunday school party on Friday evening, but don't count it as your evening off or as time with the family.

Never forget the importance of constant communication. You need to know what satisfies and what frustrates your loved ones, and your family needs to know that you're interested and that you care. If you are married, you need to know what is going on in your spouse's career. If you have children, every school open house is more important than any meeting of the building and grounds committee. Don't let the church get in the way of your Christian responsibilities.

In the family, we glimpse unconditional love. There we find the encouragement and sustenance we need to see us through the tough times, and there we accept the greatest opportunity to love and to be loved. Pastors who nurture happiness in their personal lives are far more likely to experience satisfaction in their vocation.

As I sit at the bedside of many people near the end of their earthly lives, I hear their reflections when the whispers of mortality can no longer be ignored. I have listened as they reminisce through decades of memories, drawing to a close the final chapters. Through laughter and tears, they tell their stories, remembering the great and joyous moments, reliving the painful sorrows. Their stories reveal the sharp distinction between transient attainments and eternal treasures.

And no one who finishes that course of faith looks down the arches of the years to say wistfully, "I only wish I had spent *less* time with my family." The final lament is always the opposite.

Do make time for your family!

Outside Involvements

Keeping Perspective

I have become all things to all men, that I might by all means save some.   *—I Corinthians 9:22b*

Many ministers could rephrase Paul's words: "I have become one thing, a pastor, to one small group, a church, that I might by few means save a handful."

Pastors with well-rounded interests strengthen their ministry in the community. The narrower our range of outside involvements, the scarcer is our contact with the nonchurch people who need us most.

Pastors without other involvements confuse the church with the world, thinking that everyone thinks and talks and works just as those in church do. They lose touch. They think the most important issue in the entire community is the lack of a junior-high Sunday school teacher.

Outside involvements give insight into the way nonchurch people are addressing some of the same needs the church addresses. The pastor learns how other people view the church and becomes better equipped to attract and involve newcomers.

The pastor's outside activities increase the visibility and witness of the church; many new members first come to church because they meet the pastor in the community. And skills that pastors develop in community work prove helpful back at the church.

Even when such activities serve no useful purpose for the church, pastors need to pursue outside interests for emotional well-being and diversion, and to avoid burnout. Pastors need some friends who are not church members, some organizations that are not religious, and hobbies that draw them away from ministry.

The motivations for outside commitments are as varied as the opportunities. You may attend lunch meetings of civic clubs or other organizations. But don't just go out of a sense of obligation. If you do not enjoy your current outside activities, drop them. Choose activities you find enjoyable and rewarding, and get involved. Do something that offers diversion from your work and encourages new friendships.

Many pastors are amateur experts. They serve their parishes well, but work extensively in ornithology or local history or painting, and they gather with other people who share that interest. Not everything you do with your life must serve a high and holy purpose. Many pastors help with tennis tournaments or organize chess clubs.

Occasionally church leaders fear that pastors will neglect their church work if they take on nonchurch responsibilities, so assure the people that your first mission is to serve the church. But while you always serve the church *first,* you cannot serve the church *only.* Describe the benefit to the church when your contact with nonchurch people increases. Mention your own personal need to have more than one focus. The members need church involvement as a diversion from *their* work, while you need something *besides* church work as a diversion from yours.

In addition to outside interests to refresh the mind, one also needs ways to refresh the body.

Many books describe the way spiritual well-being affects physical health. Faith positively influences physical troubles, and the opposite is also true: Physical health positively affects spiritual well-being. If we are easily fatigued or emotionally strung out, we simply cannot tackle complex problems. Our perceptions, our capacity for decisions, our tolerance for stress—all are affected by exercise and rest.

Re-creation

Renewing the Spirit by Refreshing the Body

Come away by yourselves to a lonely place, and rest a while.
—*Mark 6:31*

Our work drains us emotionally and depletes us physically. But consider how little exertion the pastoral ministry requires. Most days involve such strenuous exertion as sitting behind the desk, answering the phone, shaking hands, getting in and out of the car, kneeling for Communion. Our bodies require far more activity to stay well-tuned.

Through physical exercise, the machinery runs more efficiently. Stress is reduced and the heart rate is lowered. We breathe more easily, feel less tired during the day and more settled at night. Those who exercise regularly need less sleep and sleep more soundly.

Exercise re-creates us spiritually. A long evening walk or an early-morning tennis match helps us integrate the experiences of the day. Even when my body doesn't need it, my soul does. I need the time to ruminate, to think things through. When my blood is running and my breathing is strong and steady, my mind flows easily through the experiences of the day. The most difficult troubles are seen from a fresh perspective.

Physical exertion stimulates the creative process. Many

of my best sermon ideas come during evening walks. Something about exercise causes the imagination to run wild. In my study, I pump as hard as I can to draw water from the well, but during exercise, ideas fall like refreshing rain. This is the true definition of inspiration. Give the body something to do, and the mind and soul open up.

In generations past, preachers answered God's call while continuing to earn their living at making tents, harvesting grain, weaving cloth. Physical exertion was a part of everyday life. And during repetitive tasks, preachers found time to ruminate and receive. Perplexing puzzles were considered and reconsidered; encounters with parishioners were rehearsed in the mind; theological complexities were thought through thoroughly. Today we still need those times, but the only way to acquire them is through intentional and regular exercise.

One study suggests that regular exercise helps with depression more than do many types of therapy. And it helps to dissipate anger. We bring home all kinds of emotional turmoil. Recurring thoughts and unresolved feelings can easily dominate our life, but our problems appear less immediate after a good workout.

So develop a regular pattern of exercise. Walking requires no skill or training and is as effective as tennis or handball. Begin simply. Create an exercise program, and you will find yourself being created anew.

Pastors also must be reminded to take days off and vacations away from the church. It is an incredible act of presumption to think that the church simply cannot survive without you for one or two days a week, or even for a week or two during the year. The Body of Christ survived for two thousand years before you arrived.

You need time away, and the church needs time

without you. No church is stronger because the pastor never lets a meeting take place without being present. And no pastor is stronger for attending every meeting of the year.

We are not the first to think too highly of ourselves and our work. Jesus reminded his disciples that their work would not falter, that the world would still need them, even if they took a rest.

When they returned from their travels and their teaching, Jesus said, "Come away by yourselves to a lonely place, and rest awhile." He knew that adequate rest does not weaken our work, but enhances it. Rest does not distract our spirit, but strengthens it. God's grace comes through our work, but also through days off and time away.

Questions for Reflection

In what ways do you bring your job and your role home with you?

If you are married, what vision of your work does your spouse receive through you?

How do your family members know of your active interest in their affairs? Twenty-five years from now, how would you like them to characterize your relationship? What are you doing today to move in that direction?

What outside involvements mean most to you? Who sees you outside your role as pastor?

How have nonchurch friendships blessed you?

Based on your current habits, how do you predict your physical health twenty-five years from now?

What are you doing about it?

The Joys and Satisfactions of Ministry

I remind you to rekindle the gift of God that is within you through the laying on of my hands. —II Timothy 1:6

I n seminary, I worked at a hospital to complete a unit of Clinical Pastoral Education. One day the emergency-room nurse called me to console a man whose wife had suffered a heart attack. We were sitting together in the small, poorly lit consultation room, knees nearly touching, when the doctor arrived to inform him that his wife had died.

The man was seventy years old. He and his wife had risen that day, enjoyed a pleasant and ordinary breakfast, and then left to go shopping at a nearby mall. She knew of no health problems and experienced no warning signs. They had no way to foresee that the day which had started so happily and naturally would end so suddenly and tragically.

I asked him if I could call his pastor. He told me they attended no church and had no pastor. I asked if I could call someone he worked with. He answered that he was retired from another city and worked with no one locally. I asked if I could call a neighbor. He said that he and his wife had lived in their apartment only three years and knew no one who lived around them. He could think of no one to help.

At the end of our conversation, the man signed the final papers, gathered his wife's eyeglasses and wedding ring into a small plastic bag and walked out through the emergency-room door entirely alone, to face his grief without the consolation of faith or friends.

Life is not meant to be that way. God does not create us to live alone or intend for us to face life's greatest challenges without help. Jesus Christ died so that we might be reconciled to one another and to God. God creates us to live in community, sustaining one another in love, glorifying God through our love and service. Life in Christ—abundant life—is God's intention for every one of us. We are knit together into the community of faith for strength and sustenance.

The incident I just described was repeated, with slight variations, every week that summer. If the demographers are correct, nearly 60 percent of the people in any community have no relationship with the church. Nearly 60 percent cannot name a pastor who knows them, do not know the sustaining stories of the Christian faith, have not experienced the joy of Christian community, have not discovered the meaning that comes through serving others and God. Wherever you live and work, 60 percent of the people around you do not have the theology, the faith, the prayer life, or the companionship that offer the greatest spiritual resources ever known to help us through times of need.

People need the Lord. People need one another. People need the life-giving faith and hope and love that Christ offers through the church. God has met our highest hopes and deepest needs through Christ, and the love of the church as the Body of Christ is destined to fulfill those needs today, in ways that no social club or sports association or therapist's couch can completely address.

But God has called men and women to places of responsible leadership, using their gifts to provide to people's spiritual needs. The task is awesome; it can be all-consuming. And we must learn to be satisfied with good work that is yet unfinished; it is more than you and I can ever hope to accomplish. But God uses our inadequate best, promising that when we respond to the call, God will be with us through it all—good times and bad.

We dare not lose touch with our call. Everything else may be fuzzy, but our relationship to Jesus Christ, from whom we derive our essential purpose, must be worked on, nurtured, kept clearly in focus.

If I am devoted only to myself, the receding nature of my own ambitions will cause me to run myself ragged. If I am devoted only to humanity, I will soon fall exhausted from the overwhelming size of the task. If I am devoted only to material gain and physical comfort, I will wear myself out trying to feed insatiable appetites. But if I love Jesus Christ personally and passionately, derive my sense of mission from his, and my sense of direction from him, I will be able to serve humanity, even through painful rejection and defeat.

The ministry of Christ needs talented leaders, hard workers from all backgrounds—people with genuine motivations who are willing to respond positively to God's call. The ministry needs people to take on the great challenges of our day, using their experiences, their training, their abilities in obedience to God. But most of all, Christ's ministry needs people willing to go through the daily drudgery of a disciple, dedicated to the most ordinary tasks, working to bring people together to love and serve one another.

I have enjoyed my early years in the ordained ministry, and although this book mentions many struggles and setbacks, they are the sand grains around which pearls are formed. The doubts and difficulties fade toward obscurity beside the love I have experienced, the encouragement I have received, the satisfactions I have enjoyed. I might have been just as happy in another vocation, but I do not think I could have been happier. Answering God's call is among the greatest privileges of life, and the times of testing are marked also by enjoyable people and satisfying work.

In these last few chapters, I have made specific suggestions about ways to keep in touch with the call as the life-sustaining vision, the central motivation for ministry. Those measures may sound time consuming or too self-centered. You may think they show too little regard for the demands of the church, but if we do not take care of ourselves, we have nothing to offer others.

Are these suggestions possible? They are not only possible, but absolutely necessary. And they are so simple that I have struggled with the fear that they will be viewed as simple-minded and quickly set aside as too casual an answer to the complexities of vocational doubt. Perhaps it is their inherent simplicity that has caused these disciplines to be so rarely mastered, so commonly overlooked, and so terribly neglected. Every pastor offers hungry parishioners recipes for spiritual nourishment that include prayer, community, study, and rest. These suggestions merely encourage pastors to feast at the same banquet they serve up for others.

Many of the suggestions dovetail nicely. A reading group with other clergy keeps your study current while bringing you together with other ministers. Some people use their morning jog or evening walk as their time of prayer. Many see journal keeping as an essential task during weekly study time.

Work to develop some way to keep in touch with the deeper motivations. Without intentional effort to renew the spirit, a fulfilling and effective ministry is impossible. Choose the mixture of tasks that is most relevant to your own context. You will greatly enrich your spirit and increase your effectiveness.

Testing the call to ministry—with what attitude can we work well and grow steadily? I know deep within my heart that the ministry needs more than I can ever offer. But I trust that the God who has called me is with me and promises to use my inadequate best to proclaim the gospel and create the Kingdom. For that reason, I can continue my journey and "press on toward the goal for the prize of the upward call of God in Christ Jesus" (Phil. 3:14).